A T·E·X·A·S
FAMILY'S COOKBOOK

Joseph Lowery

with Donald R. Counts, M.D. and

Kathryn O'C. Counts

WEATHERVANE BOOKS
New York

To my father,

JOSEPH H. LOWERY,

and my grandmother

CLARA H. LOWERY

This 1988 edition is published by Weathervane Books, distributed
by Crown Publishers, Inc., 225 Park Avenue South, New York,
New York 10003, by arrangement with Texas Monthly Press

Manufactured in the United States of America

Library of Congress Cataloging-in-Publication Data

Lowery, Joseph.
    A Texas family's cookbook / Joseph Lowery with Donald R.
Counts, and Kathryn O'C Counts.
    Reprint. Originally published: Austin, Texas : Texas Monthly
Press, 1986.
    Includes index.
    ISBN 0-517-65357-5
    1. Cookery (Natural foods)   2. Cookery—Texas.   I. Counts,
Donald R., 1945-   II. Counts, Kathryn O'C., 1943-
        III. Title.
TX741.L69 1988
641.5—dc19   87-29607
                                                            CIP

ISBN 0-517-65357-5

h g f e d c b a

CONTENTS

ACKNOWLEDGMENTS

For inspiration and support, I wish to thank my family (especially Marianne Lowery), the Reverend Jack W. Cole, Kathy Massey, the Reverend William Daniels, Anne C. Daniels, Dianne Ezernack, Stephanie Holt, and Mary Faulk Koock. For suggestions and contributions, we are indebted to Ann Clark, Donald R. Wertz, James C. Cranfill, Brenda Higgie, Brian Sursky, David Lowery, Pamela Navarez, Janice Beeson, Terry Tannen, Carl Manz, Lorel Scott, Lynda McLaughlin, Lucinda Hutson, and Mary Cook. Carrlyn Miller, who organized us and kept us going, gave invaluable assistance in the preparation of the manuscript, as did Pam Hardwick, Wendy Wingfield, Mary Ellen Dennison, Chris Kindschi, and Kathy Underwood. A special thank-you to Diane Roberts for her never-ending affection and enthusiasm.

PREFACE

America has long been blessed with marvelous natural foodstuffs and excellent regional cooks with fine specialties. These talented individuals often developed their skills without any formal training. Our puritanical background has perhaps restricted our perception of art in general. Certainly, activities producing as much sensuous pleasure as eating had to be viewed with suspicion. With our traditional training, the domestic or professional cook has been rather colorless at best and nonexistent at worst. The availability of cooking schools for amateurs and high-quality programs for professionals at culinary institutes was very limited until quite recently. Of course, there were professionals who acquired formal training, but many learned their business through a career spent moving from one kitchen to another. Staying only long enough to study a particular chef's skills and (often boring) menus, an aspiring cook soon moved on for the next phase of an education.

There were, however, good American cookbooks like *Joy of Cooking, The Fannie Farmer Cookbook, The James Beard Cookbook,* and others. In 1961 came the publication of volume 1 of *Mastering the Art of French Cooking*, by Julia Child, Louisette Bertholle, and Simone Beck. It was quite unlike most French cookbooks of the time, which were written by French chefs in French, then translated into English, and assumed expertise on the part of the reader. *Mastering the Art of French Cooking* assumed little and explained much. At the same time, in the early sixties, an American president and First Lady were being served by *le maître-cuisinier de France,* René Verdon. French cuisine became popular, chic, and accessible. Due to such step-by-step books as *Mastering the Art* and to the work of modern culinary pioneers such as James Beard, M.F.K. Fisher, and Craig Claiborne, Americans began to embrace French cooking. We were able to attempt, successfully, beautiful French classics, and we learned not to be disheartened by failures. As Julia Child once said on her television show, "Serve your mistakes—they'll never know." This led to a vastly broadened appreciation of French cooking. Americans have become much more sophisticated in their native cookery as well. This grafting of classic techniques onto good home cooking is a major milestone in our national culinary history.

Another important event affecting our cooking was the natural foods movement of the sixties and seventies. It seems likely that America's growing dissatisfaction with mass-produced food can be traced to the sensibilities of those times. Our delightful preoccupation with fresh produce and other "gourmet" American products was nurtured by this movement. Granted, the early experimenting often produced coarse results, but as a succeeding generation of health-conscious cooks has discovered, a dish may be quite wholesome and nutritious, yet profit greatly from the application of refined techniques. The improvements in taste, texture, and especially appearance can be quite exciting. In recent years the availability of international ingredients, cookware, and recipes has also seriously influenced us.

This is a modern American cookbook that is primarily American-oriented, uses nutritious products, and yet is based on classic cooking techniques. It is written for the awakening American cook who appreciates not only good taste and sound nutrition but also the joy of art in the kitchen.

This book, then, is really about us and our very much developing and continuing American art of cooking —a book that lovingly reflects our regional traditions of family home cooking. We also explore the new American cooking, refining familiar dishes with classic preparation techniques and an increased awareness of health and nutrition. Perhaps this "new" cooking is simply a deeper appreciation of our own heritage and an awakening to our potential of producing a cuisine truly global in scope and authority.

NUTRITIONAL FOREWORD

A few general medical concepts should be discussed briefly to assist you in increasing your awareness of foods, in deciding whether to consume certain foods in moderation or avoid them completely. By "avoid," I do not mean totally eliminating these substances all at once. The road to sensible eating takes many steps, so I do not expect—nor should you expect of yourself—total compliance with all of my suggestions. But as you begin to apply those suggestions for better food management, the developing learning process becomes exciting as well as challenging. (Probably the most difficult challenge is eating with friends in their homes or in restaurants. Here the lessons to learn are kindness to the host and elimination of the least sensible foods.)

The entire concept of eating sensibly must remain fun and rewarding or it becomes just another diet. As you probably realize, crash diets do not work. A constant, steady change of dietary intake must occur for weight to be lost and/or redistributed from fat to protein (muscle). Diets of a few weeks' duration allow you to lose water and a few pounds of muscle, but very little fat tissue. Fat loss occurs as a response to a decrease in caloric intake and an increase in exercise. Our body fat is a storehouse of usable energy. When the body senses that a hibernation, or diet, is about to begin, it brings into play protective mechanisms that call for water and muscle to be utilized before fat stores of energy are consumed. Thus a quick two-week diet results in water loss, some protein wasting, and only a negligible effect on fat deposits. In fact, the percentage of body fat by weight is usually raised, so when the diet is discontinued and water is restored, the end result is overall weight gain in the fat cells, with mild to moderate protein wasting. With repeated dieting, expect muscle wasting, atrophy, and larger deposits of fat stores.

To avoid this scenario, simply decide to eat in moderation and exercise aerobically. This sensible approach to losing weight or just becoming more physically fit can save you time, money, and enormous effort.

It is time to introduce the word "vegetarian" into the framework of the sensible eating program. This word connotes strange images to most people, especially to heavy consumers of red meat, cheese, eggs, bacon, and grease in general. But a sensible, balanced vegetarian program introduces healthier proteins, with less saturated fat, than those provided by red meat. Vegetarians carry ten to twenty pounds less excess fat, have lower cholesterol and triglyceride levels, and have fewer heart attacks, cancers, strokes, and degenerative diseases. In short, vegetarians are healthier people. A diet that is 60 to 70 percent complex carbohydrates (grains, beans, and vegetables), 20 to 25 percent protein (animal or grain-legume-vegetable), and 5 to 10 percent fat (a combination of monosaturated, polyunsaturated, and unsaturated) is sensibly balanced. You do not need meat every day, especially red meat, and you certainly do not need meat at every meal. Your body does need protein, but in much smaller quantities than we as Texas-Americans were taught. The principle of the healthy vegetarian diet is grain and vegetable combinations complemented by either dairy products or legumes for a complete, usable protein source. When considering lighter foods remember oriental cuisines, consisting of soups and vegetable combinations with strips of meat serving as entrées. A few ounces of white meat (fish or fowl) can serve several people. For the red meat eaters, thin slices of beef can satisfy the craving for a large, juicy steak.

As a reformed red meat consumer, I must admit I found it difficult to give up eating those strips of greasy bacon in the morning, but with persistence the taste for red meat slowly changes. I was reared in Fort Worth during the forties and fifties on delicious Southern cooking that included bacon, ham, or sausage for breakfast, a hamburger or cold cuts for lunch, and steak (grilled, broiled, or chicken-fried) every evening. I still crave cream gravy and chicken-fried steak. What do I do about these grease cravings? Mostly I ignore them, but occasionally I give in and sample bites from my wife's plate. I justify it as my "vitamin G" intake for the month. So, sure, there are ways of cheating on any program, and that is why we use the phrase "sensible eating program," not "diet." We can occasionally satisfy a craving without "going off a diet." But we can do this only when eating sensibly has become a way of life.

Donald R. Counts, M.D.

GENERAL COOKING INFORMATION

RECOMMENDED TOOLS AND EQUIPMENT

Because of the many cookware stores in America today, a vast panorama of culinary equipment is offered to the cooking public.

In cooking, as in many other situations, good tools do make a difference. And as usual, quality can be expensive. But if you approach outfitting your kitchen with some practical forethought, a basic collection of kitchen tools can be within many budgets.

Buy items you think you will use and avoid fads. Buy the best you can afford, but remember that price alone is not always a sign of a tool's usefulness.

Start with a few good tools and add to your collection whenever you can.

Knives

Take the time to hold each knife before you purchase. It should feel functional and right. Knives are the basic kitchen tool, so choose well and keep them sharp. Most important, perhaps, is a good chef's knife, 8 to 10 inches long. A 3- or 4-inch paring knife is also extremely useful. Invest in a good sharpening steel, too.

How to Sharpen a Knife
Hold the sharpening steel in your left hand, pointing it out from your body. Hold the knife in your right hand and place it against the steel as shown in figure 1a. Pull the blade toward you along the steel. As you draw the blade across the steel, move the knife so that the whole length of the blade contacts the steel (figures 1b and 1c). Repeat the process on the other side of the knife and steel (figure 1d).

Continue back and forth until the knife is sharp.

Gas or Electric?

Many people find cooking on an electric stove more difficult than cooking on a gas stove. The open flame is much easier to regulate than the flat metal burner. However, with a little experience you can get excellent results with the electric range. Always remember that electric burners are probably hotter than you think they are. So as a rule of thumb—especially when cooking sauces—cook over lower heat than you might think you need. To prepare the burner quickly, turn it to high for a minute or two and then reduce to low. And don't forget to turn off the burner when you're through cooking!

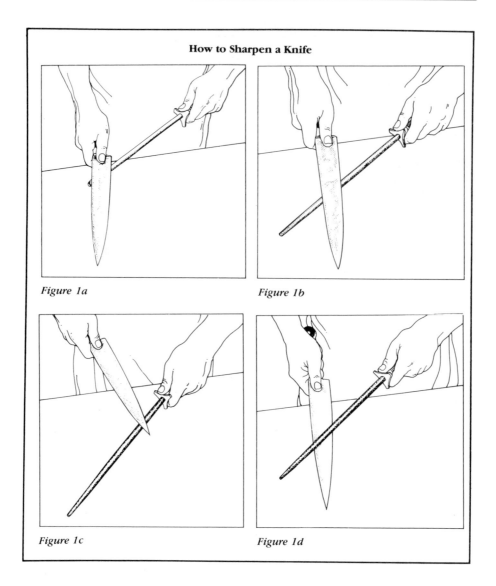

How to Sharpen a Knife

Figure 1a

Figure 1b

Figure 1c

Figure 1d

Cookware

Woks, saucepans, sauté pans, skillets, and bakeware are the workhorses of the kitchen. Copper is king, and purchase it if you can, but other styles of cookware can be just as useful.

Stainless steel, enameled cast iron, and cast iron itself are quite desirable.

Seasoning Cast-Iron Cookware
Versatile and reasonably priced, cast-iron cookware is practically indispensable, certainly for ethnic cooking

such as Creole or Mexican. Newly purchased cast-ironware must be seasoned properly before use, and older pieces should be reseasoned from time to time. To season, heat the oven to 500°, wash and dry the new cookware, then generously grease all iron surfaces with vegetable shortening. Turn the cookware upside down on a baking tray lined with foil. Bake in oven for 1 hour. Once cool, the ironware is ready for use. After each use wash and dry the pan by hand and place it in a warm oven to prevent rust. Another method is to set it on a warm burner, but take care not to leave it too long.

Incidentals
Pick your odds and ends wisely. Have what you need. If your storage space is cluttered with interesting but seldom-used tools, your cooking efficiency will be retarded. If you are just beginning, a chat with an experienced cook can save you time and money. The list that follows is a suggestion for a basic assortment.

    wooden spoons with good, sturdy
      handles
    nice metal whisks
    strainers of various sizes, including
      a chinois, or China hat (a large
      conical strainer invaluable in
      making stock)
    several rubber spatulas
    melon ballers
    zester for cutting citrus zests

    decorative molds
    at least 2 comfortably large cutting
      boards
    several sizes of colanders
    metal tongs
    Pyrex and stainless steel measuring
      cups
    old-fashioned hand pastry blender
    sifter
    stainless steel mixing bowls in
      several sizes
    vegetable peeler
    kitchen shears or scissors
    bamboo or metal steamer

Luxuries
There are many timesaving electric food devices well worth acquiring. Blenders and food processors make so many things so much quicker and easier that you should by all means include both in your kitchen. An electric mixer, especially a standing model with a bread hook attachment, will also save you much time.

An electric ice cream machine—or, if your budget allows, a sorbet machine—can help you create not only traditional frozen desserts but low-calorie, healthful dishes as well.

A pasta machine, if you love fresh pasta, is a fine idea. Juicers for making your own fruit and vegetable juices are a great source of joy.

With the right models for your needs and with proper care, these investments will reward you for years.

STOCKING THE PANTRY

When you go shopping, try to give yourself time to enjoy it. Approach

food shopping as an education, as excitement rather than a chore. Chatting with your suppliers as well as with other shoppers can increase your food knowledge in interesting ways. Become a package reader and an inquirer about unfamiliar items.

You may find yourself shopping at a number of places to create the dishes in this book. Be prepared to visit not only the large familiar chains but also small produce dealers, farmers' markets, natural food stores, gourmet shops, and oriental and other ethnic markets.

Try to buy produce that is unadulterated, in season, and, if possible, locally grown. A little experience will teach you to select the best items for your needs.

The following are suggestions for nutritious items to keep on hand. Naturally, you will not buy all these things at once, but this list may give you some ideas for serving a greater variety of foods to your family.

Baked Goods

whole wheat bread crumbs
croutons
specialty crackers
hamburger buns
commercial whole-grain sandwich
    bread or homemade bread
scones
muffins
whole wheat tortillas
English muffins
occasional pies, cakes, cookies

Refrigerator Items

skim milk
acidophilus milk
half-and-half for special occasions
cream for special occasions
fruit juices
fresh fruits and berries
cheeses, meats, and eggs
low-fat yogurt
dry baking yeast
bran
wheat germ
corn germ
lecithin

unsalted soy margarine
butter
tofu (soybean curd)
sour cream
sauces and salsas
salad dressings
prepared horseradish
homemade mayonnaise
gourmet mustards
olives and peppers
pickles and relishes
jellies and jams
fresh produce
parsley, cilantro, and other fresh
    herbs

Freezer Foods

fruits and vegetables (frozen at home
    when in season)
assorted coffees
chicory
baking chocolate
pine nuts
pecans and other nuts
unsalted soy margarine or butter
fresh pastas
breads and other baked goods
seafood, poultry, and meats

prepared main dishes
glaces and demiglaces
stocks and ingredients for stocks
commercial and homemade ice
   creams and sorbets

Dry Stock

whole-grain hot and cold cereals
whole-grain and vegetable pastas
cornmeal
whole wheat, unbleached white, soy,
   and other specialty flours
brown, Texmati, and wild rice
whole barley
cracked wheat
buckwheat groats
couscous
lentils
split peas
garbanzo, white, black, and pinto
   beans
Redi-Mix (page 128)
sesame, sunflower, and pumpkin
   seeds
almonds, walnuts, and pistachios
currants and raisins
dried apricots, pineapple, papaya, and
   apples

Canned and Specialty Products

green chiles
pimientos
beans
tomato sauce
artichoke hearts
hearts of palm
white asparagus
broth (beef, chicken, clam)
bouillons

Chinese specialties (water chestnuts,
   bamboo shoots, baby corn)
water-packed tuna
sockeye salmon
olives
home-canned goods
capers
pickles

Herbs, Spices, and Flavorings

Dried leaf herbs
dill weed
chervil
oregano
tarragon
summer savory
sweet basil
sage
rosemary
thyme
bay leaves
cilantro (coriander)
saffron
mint

Peppers and Peppercorns
paprika
ground cayenne
coarsely ground red chile
pink, green, white, and black
   peppercorns
ground black and white pepper

Dried Preparations
filé powder
garlic powder
chili powder
five-spice powder
curry powder
garam masala
turmeric
ground coriander seed

ground cumin (comino) seed
dry mustard
ground kelp

Whole Seeds
poppy seed
white and black sesame seeds
white and black mustard seeds
fennel seed
caraway seed
dill seed
celery seed
cumin (comino) seed
juniper berries

Spices and Extracts
whole and ground nutmeg
whole and ground cloves
whole and ground allspice
whole and ground cardamom
whole, ground, and candied ginger
ground cinnamon
whole vanilla beans
vanilla extract
almond extract
orange extract
lemon extract
ginger extract
mint extract

Condiments and Vinegars
Worcestershire sauce
tamari soy sauce
preserves
syrups
herb and fruit vinegars
Tabasco sauce

Cold Pressed Oils and Fats

sesame oil
safflower oil
sunflower oil
extra virgin olive oil
corn oil

nut oils
vegetable shortening

Sweeteners

honey
molasses
maple syrup
raw turbinado sugar
beet or cane sugar
fructose
aspartame (Equal)
apple, white grape, and other fruit
   juices

Leavenings and Thickenings

low-sodium baking powder
baking soda
cream of tartar
arrowroot
cornstarch
pureed couscous
gelatin

Cooking Wines

dry white vermouth
white table wine
red table wine
dry sherry
Madeira wine
marsala wine

Delicacies and Oddities

seaweeds
dried mushrooms and fungi
dried lily buds

Beverages

natural fruit and vegetable juices
spring waters

fine coffees (including decaffeinated)
quality teas (including decaffeinated)
chamomile, peppermint, and herbal
teas

ENTERTAINING: SUGGESTED MENUS

Should you hire a professional caterer? If the number of guests or the significance of the occasion warrants it, yes. A good caterer can give you time to enjoy and experience the truly memorable occasion. However, for parties not quite so grand, you will enjoy creating your own. One basic tip: don't overextend yourself. It is very easy to imagine a great deal more than you can produce. A large dinner party is not the occasion to experiment with some new and elaborate recipe. Do try to be fresh and innovative in menu and presentation. Plan your party carefully and give ample thought to timing, temperature of dishes, storage, service pieces, special equipment, staff (if necessary), and cleanup. With some attention to detail, you can make your affair pleasant not only for your guests but for yourself as well.

The 11 menus in this section are intended to stir the imagination, although realities like timing, calories, and—in the instance of vegetarian menus—complementary protein combinations have been taken into account. When planning your own menus, try to consider the appropriateness of each element. Don't overfantasize.

Informal Dinners

Meatless Menus

Pear, Walnut, and Watercress Salad
  (page 84)
Creamy Cauliflower Soup With Corn
  and Rice (page 61)
Nannie's Rolls (page 179)
fresh fruit and cheese

Cold Creamy Peach Soup (page 77)
Polenta Pie (page 125)
Saffron Brown Rice (page 122)
English Peas (page 110)
Honey Custard (page 209)

Potato-Leek Soup (page 63)
Bean and Rice Creole Casserole
  (page 124)
Carrot and Raisin Salad (page 83)
Whole Wheat Scones (page 183)
Baked Apples With Currants (page
  207)

Poultry Menu

Waldorf Cocktail (page 33)
Hot and Sour Soup (page 70)
Sautéed Chicken Breasts With Braised
  Julienne of Vegetables (page 147)
Lentil-Grain Duet (page 124)
Raspberry Tart (page 205)

Veal Menu

Low-Sodium Caesar Salad (page 81)
Broiled Veal Cutlets With Mango
    (page 158)
String Beans With Flavored Butters
    (page 104)
Curried Barley Pilaf (page 123)
Strawberry Fluff Sorbet (page 209)

Seafood Menu

Gazpacho (page 74)
Grilled Fresh Catfish (page 171)
Snow Peas With Fresh Ginger
    (page 111)
Corn on the Cob (page 107)
Gingerbread (page 196)

Formal Seated Dinners

Meatless Menu

Fresh Celery Hearts (page 32)
Sopa de Ajo (page 71)
Tofu Amandine (page 125)
Garbanzo Bean Salad (page 84)
Spaghetti Squash (page 115) with
    Pesto Sauce (page 132)
Family Heirloom Tea Cakes
    (page 191)
Mint Leaf Tea (page 215)

Shrimp Menu

Stuffed Baked Mushrooms (page 31)
Warm Consommé of Raspberry
    (page 77)
Shrimp in Paprika Sauce With Pasta
    Primavera (page 166)

French Bread Sticks (page 175)
Chocolate Mousse (page 208)

Veal and Game Bird Menu

Egg-Lemon Soup With Barley
    (page 75)
Game Bird Salad (page 86)
Roast Veal With Vegetable Sauce
    (page 157)
Basic Baked Potato (page 112)
Texas Honey Pecan Pie (page 204)

Buffet Dinners

Texas Fiesta Menu

Texas Liquid Gold Margarita
    (page 217)
tortilla chips and fresh salsas
Guacamole (page 81)
Fajitas (page 159)
slices of fresh fruit

Southwestern New Year's Menu

Texas Caviar (page 33)
Mother's Cheese Puffs (page 34)
Jicama Mexicana (page 32)
freshly boiled shrimp with Seafood
    Cocktail Sauce (page 52) and
    Chipotle Mayonnaise (page 92)
Stir-Fried Vegetables in a Wok
    (page 118)
fruit and cheese
All-American Apple Pie (page 202)

COOKING WITH CHILDREN

Private cooking schools came of age in America in the 1970s. In many areas, all over the country, cooking instruction is available not only in all styles and disciplines but for all age groups as well. Americans are taking to cooking for fun as never before.

For several years I enjoyed the challenge of teaching children's cooking classes. As a member of the staff of an Austin cooking school, I shared with others the responsibility of instructing budding chefs aged 6 to 12. These classes were remarkably successful in terms of providing a satisfying and stimulating experience for most of the young students. Some of the children showed a marked proficiency in cooking and advanced quickly. All levels of cooks, however, can experience the most important aspect of children's cooking: basic confidence. A child who knows that

he or she can handle a knife, raw food, and heat is a child who can feed himself or herself, and therefore a child who is better equipped to cope with other responsibilities.

Pick happy times to cook with your children. Do not attempt any project if you are hurried or tense— it ruins it. Never instruct your young chefs to hurt themselves: "Don't do that; you'll cut yourself." They will! Instead, try to monitor the activity while giving positive instructions: "We don't cut ourselves because we hand each other the knife this way." Let your children handle knives often, and carefully develop their awareness and concentration. They will be safe cooks, if not future executive chefs. Pick realistic recipes, and be unfailingly positive about the results.

TECHNIQUES

Blanching

Blanching is used to tenderize and intensify color of cold vegetables; for hot dishes, it is a method of precooking. To blanch vegetables, bring 3 quarts of water to a rapid boil. Drop in chopped vegetables and reduce to simmer. Cook 1 to 5 minutes, depending on the vegetable. Remove from hot water and plunge into a large bowl of ice water. This sets the color and stops the cooking process. Drain and dry. Serve cold, perhaps on a crudité platter. To warm, reimmerse in cooking water and simmer for 30 seconds, or sauté with a flavored butter or oil.

Butter

To soften cold butter quickly to use in a recipe, grate and allow to stand 2 minutes.

Celery

Slice off the bottom 1 to 2 inches of the celery bunch and wash the stalks separately. Remove strings by breaking the celery stalk toward the back and pulling away the strip of celery or by peeling with a vegetable peeler. Older leafy sections may be bitter but are useful as garnish. Use outer stalks for cooking and inner stalks for eating raw.

Cheese

Always grate cheese cold. Room-temperature cheese tastes much better, but it is difficult to grate.

Chicken

Boiling. To boil chicken for eating or for use in other recipes, always place it in water that is already simmering or boiling. This will cook the chicken quickly, leaving flavor and nutrients intact. (To make stock you start cooking the chicken in cold water, leaching out the flavor into the liquid, leaving the meat useless.)

Cubing. To avoid the unsightly ragged look of cooked chicken cubed with a knife, cut the pieces with scissors or kitchen shears. This quick, simple technique produces beautiful, uniform results.

Chile Peppers

It is an excellent idea to wear thin latex gloves when working with chiles. Be very careful not to rub your face or eyes—serious pain can result.

Roasting. Method 1: Spread peppers in 1 layer in a cast-iron skillet and heat to medium low. Stir occasionally with a wooden spoon until skin is charred but still delicate and tender.

Method 2: Spread peppers on a baking sheet and place under the broiler. Turn frequently until evenly charred.

Method 3: Impale pepper on a skewer or fork and hold it in the flame of a gas burner. Turn until charred, as with the other methods.

Skinning. Place hot roasted peppers in a damp towel and fold into a bundle. Allow peppers to sweat 15 to 20 minutes. Remove from towel and carefully peel away the cellophanelike skin. Cut out stems and gently scrape out seeds with the end of a spoon. The peppers can be used immediately or stored up to a week in the refrigerator, or several months in the freezer.

Eggs

Hard-boiled. Place room-temperature eggs in a small saucepan and cover with tap water. Bring to a boil over medium-high heat, then turn off heat and cover pan. Allow to sit 10 to 15 minutes. Rinse under cold water and peel.

Separating. You should reserve one copper bowl exclusively for the purpose of beating egg whites. Use two other bowls for the separating process, one for the yolks and one for cleaning each individual egg white.

Break the eggs one at a time. Using the shell to retain the yolk, let the white fall into the cleaning bowl and then place the yolk in the yolk bowl. Carefully examine and clean the white, making sure that it contains no particles of yolk, shell, grease, fat, or dirt. Then place it in the copper bowl. Rinse out the cleaning bowl and begin anew for the next egg.

Fish

To select fish, first inquire about freshness, then observe the fish. With whole fish, look for a clean overall appearance, pink gills, bright, clear eyes, and a fresh smell. In fillets, check for a tight, smooth texture, a bright sheen, and a clean smell. Ask the fishmonger to put the fish on ice for carrying home with you.

Frozen Desserts

To prepare frozen desserts without an ice cream freezer or sorbet machine, mix the ingredients in a large mixing bowl, cover with plastic wrap, and freeze for 30 minutes. Then remove the bowl from the freezer and mix thoroughly with an electric mixer. Return the bowl to the freezer for another 30 minutes. Mix again and chill until needed. Remove dessert from freezer 15 to 30 minutes before serving.

Fruit

To prevent the discoloration of freshly sliced apples, pears, bananas, avocados, and so forth, toss the cut fruit with an acidic fruit juice. Lemons, limes, oranges, grapefruit, and pineapples all work well. Avoid chemical products made for this purpose.

For tender sections of citrus fruit, first slice off the ends of the fruit. Set it on one end and, holding the knife horizontally, make downward cuts around the sides of the fruit, slicing off the peel, white, and outer membrane with each stroke. Then, with a very sharp knife, separate the sections by making two vertical cuts at each division, so that the membrane on each side is cut away from the pulp.

Garlic

Always use different cutting boards for pungent vegetables like garlic and onions and sweet things like oranges and fruit. After handling raw garlic, wash your hands with soap and cold water. Hot water will set the odor.

Whole. Whole garlic *pods* may be roasted or used in vinegars and need only to be washed. When you use whole garlic *cloves,* remove the paperlike skin and cut the stem away.

Sliced. Peel cloves and take off stems. Then cut either lengthwise or crosswise in thin slices.

Mashed. Lay the blade of a large knife flat against each garlic clove and give it a hard blow with the heel of your hand. Remove the skin and stem. Still using the side of the knife, mash each clove again to release more of the aromatic oils.

Minced. Peel, destem, and mash garlic as above, chop finely with a very sharp knife, then continue to mash and mince. Mashing releases flavor that mincing doesn't.

Pureed. Best done in a blender or food processor. Drop peeled and destemmed garlic cloves into blender or food processor while machine is running. It helps to add a little liquid or oil.

Grilling

Clean the grill with a wire brush both before and after use. Light a charcoal grill at least 1 hour ahead of time so that it is very hot. Before cooking, brush the grill with oil, then put the meat on the grill at an angle. Move it to another hot portion of grill at an angle complementary to the first angle, to form diamond char patterns. Repeat this process with the other side of the meat. When the meat is done, allow the grill to burn off the cooking juices for easier cleaning.

The renowned French chef Jacques Pepin asserts that natural wood charcoal produces significantly lower amounts of tar on cooked meat than processed briquets.

Julienne of Vegetables

To cut a carrot into julienne strips, first wash and peel it and cut it into 2-inch lengths. Slice the pieces lengthwise, taking care not to allow the carrot to roll, then slice further into thin, matchlike pieces (figure 2). Handle other vegetables similarly.

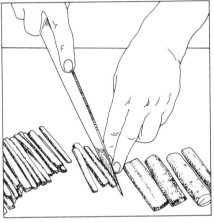

Figure 2

Leeks

Leeks, known as the poor man's asparagus, have long been a staple of continental cooking and are now available in American markets. They must be carefully cleaned before use.

Remove wilted or yellowed leaves from stalks and slice leeks in half lengthwise. Then cut into 1/4-inch-thick pieces. Soak the pieces in a large bowl of cool water for 10 to 15 minutes, then remove them carefully so as not to stir up the sand that has settled in the bottom of the bowl. Place the leeks in a colander and rinse very, very thoroughly. Allow them to drain for a few moments, then pat dry with towels or spin dry

Figure 3

in salad spinner. Cleaned, dry leeks
may be chopped further if desired
(figure 3).

Lettuce

To wash lettuce, remove the outer
leaves and cut off the bottom of the
stem so that all leaves are separate.
Soak in cool water, rinse under running water, and spin dry in a salad
spinner. Then store in a locking plastic bag with a folded paper towel to
absorb moisture. Keep refrigerated.

Mushrooms

Only very dirty mushrooms should
be washed. If possible, wipe or brush
the mushrooms clean. If they must be
washed, dry them quickly afterward.
Do not soak.

Toss sliced or quartered mushrooms with fresh lemon juice and allow to sit 30 to 60 minutes. Lemon
juice will bleach mushrooms and
lend a subtle flavor, making them
more savory eaten raw with a salad
or cooked with other ingredients.

Onions

An onion may be peeled and
chopped quickly and efficiently. Cut
off the stem end, then cut the onion
in half, slicing from the stem down
through the root bunch, known as
the chef's moustache (figure 4a).
Starting from the stem end, peel away
the paper and outer skin. Lay each
onion half flat on the cut side. Holding it from the root end, make thin
horizontal cuts (⅛ to ¼ inch apart)
from the stem end to, but not through,
the root (figure 4b). Then make similar vertical cuts, being careful to cut
to, but not through, root side of onion
(figure 4c). Carefully hold the root
side of the onion and begin slicing
vertically across the stem end toward
the root end, which will produce perfect cubed or chopped onions (figure
4d). Horizontal and vertical cuts can
be varied to produce different sized
pieces. To mince onion, simply chop
the cubed pieces to the desired
consistency.

Parsley

Cleaning. Soak the bunch of parsley
upside down in a bowl of cool water
to remove sand and dirt. When parsley has soaked about 15 minutes, remove it and rinse under cool running
water.

Chopping. Remove the leaves from
the stems, discarding any wilted or
otherwise unacceptable pieces. Reserve stems for making stock. Place
leaves on a cutting board and chop
with a rocking motion, holding the
tip of the knife in place while moving
the handle (figures 5a and 5b). Repeat until parsley is finely chopped.

Place chopped leaves in a clean

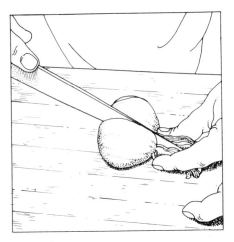

Figure 4a

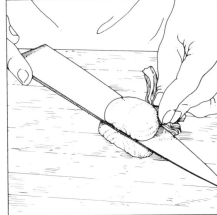

Figure 4b

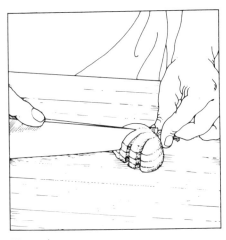

Figure 4c

Figure 4d

kitchen towel and twist as shown in figure 5c. Hold towel under running water and twist until the water that runs off is no longer green. (The chlorophyll in the parsley would otherwise color the dish.) Remove from running water and twist tightly until all moisture is exuded. Open towel and remove dry chopped parsley.

Produce

The most important reason for carefully washing your fruit and produce (beyond simply removing the dirt) is to remove chemical sprays, pesticides, and waxes. Soak produce in cool water and then rinse under cool running water. Do not assume that any commercial produce is clean. Even sprouted seeds need to be rinsed be-

Figure 5a

Figure 5b

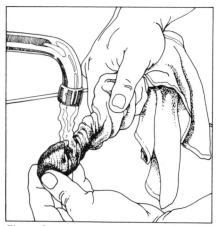

Figure 5c

fore use. Citrus fruit, on the other hand, need not be washed unless you plan to use the peel for some purpose. In that case, it should be washed and scrubbed well. If potatoes are washed and scrubbed when first brought into the kitchen, preparing them later will be much more convenient.

Pumpkin

Fresh prepared pumpkin is always preferable to canned pumpkin. Admittedly, the old method in which the raw pumpkin is cut up and boiled is a bother. But with the method described below, using fresh pumpkin can be quick and easy. You can prepare pureed pumpkin and freeze it for ready availability throughout the year.

Select firm, fresh pumpkins. One small pumpkin will do nicely for 2 or 3 recipes. However, you may wish to prepare several pumpkins at once to have plenty on hand. Wash pumpkin with warm water and dry thoroughly. Lightly oil the pumpkin and place it on a baking tray. Place the tray with the pumpkin in a 350° oven and bake for 1 hour. Pumpkin is ready when it is soft to the touch. Set the tray with the pumpkin aside to cool. While cooling, the pumpkin will begin to collapse. When it's cool enough to handle, carefully remove the stem and peel away browned skin, which should come off quite easily. Split open the pumpkin and scoop out seeds and stringy fibers. Seeds may be saved for roasting. Cut the remaining meat into chunks and finely puree in food processor or blender.

Pureed fresh pumpkin can be used in any recipe calling for canned pumpkin. This technique originated in the hills of eastern Tennessee, where many varieties of squash and pumpkin grow profusely.

Shrimp

Selecting. Check that they have a light pink to coral color (although some perfectly good shrimp are gray) and no ammonia smell.

Deveining. Remove heads from shrimp. Insert the tip of a deveining tool under the shell and run it along the vein toward the tail. This loosens the shell so that it is easily removed. Then carefully clean off any remaining pieces of vein.

Butterflying. Clean as directed above, but leave the tail section on the shrimp (don't run the deveining tool through the tail). With a sharp knife, slice through the vein area about three quarters of the way through the shrimp. The shrimp will open into a butterfly as it cooks.

Smoking

The meat smoker has considerable potential beyond the application of water-soaked wood chips to hot coals. Any flavorful liquid may be substituted for water in the pan, the aromatic steam having a subtle but definite effect on the meat. You truly are limited only by your imagination.

Soak 1 pound of mesquite or hickory wood chips in water at least 2 hours. Arrange 4 pounds of natural wood charcoal in the bottom of the smoker, leaving a space in the center. A high fire is essential to achieve and maintain the heat level necessary to cook the meat. Light the charcoal and wait at least 45 minutes for it to become fully heated. Add a quart of

boiling water to the smoker pan and place the racks of meat to be smoked in position. Add about a third of the soaked wood chips to the bed of coals, securely cover the smoker, and allow the meat to smoke the length of time directed in the recipe, turning once. Add the remaining wood chips as the smoking progresses, along with extra water as necessary.

Sour Milk

To make sour milk, add 1 teaspoon white vinegar per 1 cup milk and let stand 10 to 15 minutes.

Tofu

Tofu is usually called bean curd on oriental menus. High in protein (especially when used in combination with other foods) and low in saturated fat, this soy milk cheese continues to grow in popularity. When fresh, tofu has a thin and watery flavor, but this very blandness seems to contribute to its wonderful adaptability. Use tofu in dips, dressings, and sauces. Tofu cubes blend well in many soups and stir-fries. Serve in complementary combinations with other foods such as grains and legumes for increased available protein. You can use it to replace dairy products in some instances to create intriguing desserts. Dried tofu is available, too, for portability.

Tomatoes

Skinning. Dip tomatoes into a pan of boiling water for 3 minutes and then plunge them into ice water. The skin will split and can be easily removed with the blade of a paring knife. Remove core with the tip of the knife or a tomato shark.

Juicing and Seeding. Many recipes call for fresh tomatoes to be "peeled, juiced, and seeded." To do this quickly and effectively, peel and core fresh tomatoes and cut into quarters. Over the sink or a bowl hold the outside of each quarter against your palm and dig your fingers into the seed chamber and squeeze gently. The pulp is then ready for chopping or other preparation.

Although food presentation can be a grand and glorious art, it can also be simple and charming touches that add a little grace to your everyday menus. Begin with artful arrangements of well-cooked food.

Deft touches with sprigs of fresh herbs are always attractive. Animals and flowers carved out of fruits and vegetables certainly add a touch of sophistication. Children especially enjoy decoration.

Apple Swan

1 For practicing you will want a large piece of fruit, but swans can be made out of any size or color of apple.
2 Cut a thin slice off the bottom of the apple and set aside. Set the apple on the flat side, which will serve as its base.
3 Starting about 1 inch from the stem end, cut a wedge about ¼ inch wide from the top of the apple (figure 6a). Remove the wedge and cut another below it, just a little bigger than the first. Make a third, larger wedge and fit the 3 pieces back together on top of the bird (figure 6b). They will form the tail.
4 Repeat step 3 on each side of the apple (figure 6c). These will be the wings.
5 Place the slice from step 2 flat side down. Using your imagination and the tip of a sharp knife, cut out a swan's head and long neck. You may need to thin the slice a little or do other cosmetic surgery.
6 Cut a small hole on the top of the apple, making it large and deep enough to hold the swan's neck se-

curely. Insert 1 clove as an eye and place neck in hole.
7 Extend each set of wedges backward from the neck as far as it will go and still remain intact (figure 6d).
8 Squeeze a little lemon juice on the swan and it's ready to use.

Citrus Crown

1 Cut a deep continuous zigzag pattern around the middle of a citrus fruit. Keep the cuts even. Make sure the knife tip goes all the way through to the core on each cut (figure 7).
2 The 2 halves should separate easily. They can be further decorated with parsley, paprika, pimiento, and so forth.

Red Radish Flower

A colorful little addition that, unlike some garnishes, is easy to eat.
1 Slice the stem and root sections off a large round radish.

Figure 6a

Figure 6b

Figure 6c

Figure 6d

2 Slice directly across the middle of the top of the radish, but do not cut all the way through.

3 Repeat vertical cuts on each side of the first cut all the way to the sides of the radish. Practice will make this very easy.

4 Give the sliced radish a quarter-turn and repeat cuts (figure 8).

5 Place the radish flower in ice water to open the petals fully.

Tomato Rose

1 Start with a ripe, firm, unblemished tomato. Make your paring knife as sharp as you can get it.

2 Starting at the stem end, slice a continuous strip about ½ inch wide. Be careful; cut too thin and the skin will break, cut too thick and the skin will not roll properly.

3 When you have completely peeled

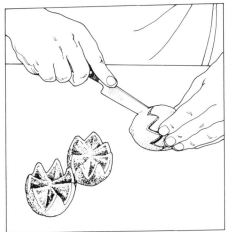

Figure 7

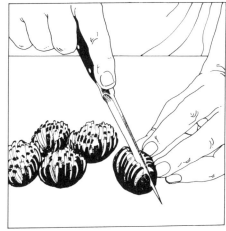

Figure 8

the tomato, reserve it for another purpose.

4 Form the rose by holding one end of the skin and rolling the rest of it layer by layer around the middle in one long spiral.

5 Set rose upright on the most stable side and use creatively.

Green Onion Flower

A very simple garnish that adds instant elegance. The size of the onion determines the size of the flower. (You can also use this technique with leeks.)

1 Select firm, healthy green onions. Wash them and slice off the root.

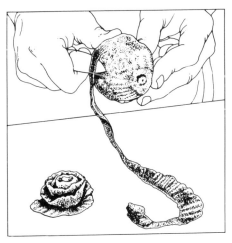

Figure 9

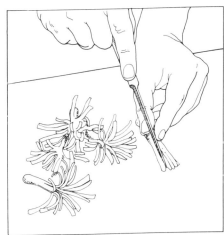

Figure 10

2 Trim greens off about 3 inches from root end.

3 With the tip of the knife, make a longitudinal cut about 1½ inches long completely through the onion. Do not cut the full length.

4 Turn onion and repeat on other side, so that onion is quartered.

5 Repeat cut twice more on opposite sides until onion has 8 cuts.

6 Drop green onion flowers into ice water until ready to use. Ice water will open the petals.

Onion Lotus

Several onion lotuses of different colors, grouped together on a platter, make a spectacular display. Purple onions are especially beautiful. This garnish is easy to make but does require delicate work.

1 Choose onions that are even and round. Any size or color will work well.

2 Peel the onion and slice off the root (figure 11a).

3 Place the onion on the flat stem end and slice in half down to ½ inch from the bottom. Make a similar cut perpendicular to the first (figure 11b).

4 Slice the onion 6 more times to make 16 divisions (figure 11c). Do not cut deeper than ½ inch from the bottom.

5 Steam or boil the onion for 1 to 2 minutes to soften it so the petals will unfold. (Purple onions seem to open more quickly and easily than white onions and need less cooking.)

6 Remove from heat and immerse in ice water until ready to use. The petals may need to be separated carefully (figure 11d).

7 Place the finished lotus on lettuce or decorate with parsley. A light coating of aspic will prevent discoloration and wilting.

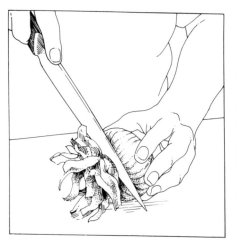

Figure 11a

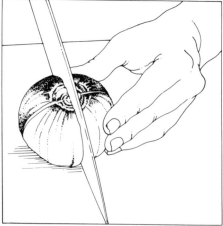

Figure 11b

Figure 11c

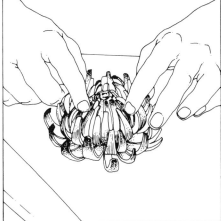

Figure 11d

ABOUT THE RECIPES

The recipes included in this book are from a number of sources, and when possible we have given credit, named inspirations, and admitted adaptations. Most recipes are not new themselves, but perhaps new in the way they are presented and combined. Many of them evolved over a period of four years when the three of us shared concepts of dietary changes to enhance a healthful approach to cooking. The philosophy throughout the book is to take good American home cooking and improve it nutritionally with an appreciation of more healthful eating habits. Second, an attempt is made to improve the dishes' textures and appearances by utilizing certain classical cooking techniques.

We certainly encourage readers to make daily use of the soup, salad, vegetable, grain, and bean recipes. Please view the meat section as one for special times, and turn more often to the lighter dishes using poultry and seafood.

We wish to acknowledge our debt to Frances Moore Lappe for her work on complementary proteins. You will definitely want to study the information contained in her book *Diet for a Small Planet*. You will also do well to explore the more healthful methods of cooking, such as braising, grilling, or broiling instead of frying, and steaming or poaching instead of boiling. We include such frying recipes as there are not to encourage frying but rather to offer longtime favorites for very occasional use.

In the matter of sweets, you should try to refrain from any daily dessert except a bit of fruit. Save your indulgences for holidays and other celebrations. We supply our cake, pastry, and other dessert recipes in this spirit. Most call for honey, fructose, or raw turbinado sugar instead of refined sugar. Aspartame (sold under the brand name of Equal) can be substituted for other sweeteners in recipes that do not require it to be heated.

In all our recipes we recommend lowered or moderate use of salt. Unfortunately, most Americans are accustomed to salt in almost everything, including soft drinks, most processed foods, entrées, vegetables, and even desserts. It is an addiction most people do not recognize. The best way to discover the difference between your addiction and your need for salt is simply to stop using any salt for 2 or 3 weeks. This respite from your salt habit allows you to taste and appreciate flavors more for what they are, and you will probably lose your desire for so much salt in a very short time. From this point, you can begin consciously to choose the amount of salt you wish to have in your diet.

Lemon juice is an excellent salt substitute. Lemon or lime juice will perk up your dish and the tartness will substitute for the salty taste.

Some of the aromatic spices and herbs, such as cumin (comino) and fresh basil, as well as pungent vegetables such as chile peppers, onions, and garlic, will give you a strong flavor sensation and help you get over the expectation of saltiness.

Condiments such as mayonnaise, ketchup, and other table sauces are very high in sodium and should be avoided. Worcestershire sauce, however, is fairly low in sodium.

If you make your own stock, you can avoid the high sodium level of commercially prepared stocks.

Baking powder and baking soda are very high in sodium. Substitute a low-sodium baking powder for the regular kind. You will need to use twice as much low-sodium baking powder as regular.

Except for special occasions, omit buttermilk in any form. Substitute the same amount of low-fat yogurt or sour milk.

Please note the techniques section that begins on page 11. It provides professional solutions to some cooking problems as well as outlining basic techniques needed for many of the recipes. Cross-references (in italics) in the recipes will direct you to this section from time to time.

Our sincere thanks to all those who contributed to the recipe development.

1

APPETIZERS AND SNACKS

★

SALMON MOUSSE

This is a large recipe for parties; however, it can be halved or quartered successfully.

YIELD: SERVES 24

¼ cup low-fat ricotta cheese
2 tablespoons low-fat milk
2 tablespoons chopped shallots
4 cups cooked fresh or canned salmon
¼ cup mayonnaise
2 teaspoons white pepper
2 tablespoons Worcestershire sauce

1 tablespoon paprika
juice of 1 lemon
2 teaspoons Tabasco sauce
1 cup dry white wine
6 tablespoons unflavored gelatin
3 egg whites
parsley for garnish

1 In a food processor, puree ricotta cheese and milk.

2 Add shallots and blend well.

3 Add salmon 1 cup at a time and continue blending.

4 Add mayonnaise, white pepper, Worcestershire sauce, paprika, lemon juice, and Tabasco sauce. Run food processor several minutes or until salmon mixture is extremely smooth and well blended.

5 While mixture is blending, place wine in a saucepan and sprinkle in gelatin. Allow to soften a minute or so, then place over very low heat for 2 or 3 minutes, whipping occasionally until gelatin dissolves. Remove from heat and set aside.

6 Whip egg whites until they form stiff peaks.

7 Remove salmon mixture from food processor and place in a large bowl. Stir in wine-gelatin mixture.

8 Fold in beaten egg whites and blend gently but thoroughly.

9 Lightly oil (1 scant teaspoon) a 6-cup decorative mold and pour mousse into mold. Chill 12 hours or longer, preferably overnight.

10 Unmold mousse by briefly placing the bottom of the mold in warm water. Invert mold onto serving platter and mousse should slide out. Decorate with parsley and vegetable flowers.

★

RABBIT PÂTÉ IN GRAPE LEAVES

YIELD: 10 SERVINGS

2 tablespoons minced shallots or green onions
2 cloves garlic

1½ pounds boned rabbit meat, uncooked
¼ cup brandy

2 eggs
1 teaspoon white pepper
1½ teaspoons thyme
1 teaspoon nutmeg
1 tablespoon Worcestershire sauce
1 tablespoon Dijon mustard

¼ cup unsalted margarine or butter
grape leaves to line mold (about 18, depending on size)
8–10 pimiento-stuffed green olives
3–5 whole bay leaves

1 Preheat oven to 350°.
2 In a food processor, combine shallots, garlic, rabbit, and brandy and blend at high speed 1 to 2 minutes.
3 Add eggs, white pepper, thyme, nutmeg, Worcestershire sauce, and Dijon mustard. Blend thoroughly.
4 Add margarine or butter and blend several minutes, until meat mixture is very smooth.
5 Lightly oil a 4-cup rectangular loaf pan or terrine.
6 Line pan with grape leaves, shiny side down. (When pâté is unmolded, the shiny side will be on the outside.) Leave enough hanging over the edge to fold over top of pâté after pan is filled.
7 Place about a third of the rabbit mixture into lined pan. Dot with half the olives and repeat until mold is full.
8 Fold over grape leaves to completely cover pâté.

9 Tap the pan against the counter several times to dislodge air bubbles.
10 Lay bay leaves over grape leaves and tightly cover pan with aluminum foil.
11 Set pan containing the pâté into a larger pan and add to the larger pan enough boiling water to come halfway up the pâté pan.
12 Place both pans in a preheated 350° oven for about 1 hour 15 minutes.
13 When done, remove pâté pan from water bath. Place a heavy weight (a brick, another terrine the same shape, a loaf pan filled with beans) on the aluminum foil to compress the pâté. Allow pâté to come to room temperature and then chill overnight, still weighted.
14 To serve, unmold pâté and cut into slices, being careful not to disturb the grape leaf covering.

★

EMPEROR'S MUSHROOM MARINADE

YIELD: SERVES 12–16

2 pounds medium or large mushrooms or mushroom caps
10–12 cloves garlic
4 ounces green peppercorns

32 ounces fine Italian or California olive oil
12 ounces champagne vinegar
½ cup brandy

1 Wipe or wash mushrooms (see *Mushrooms*).

2 Peel garlic cloves and slice thinly. Mash green peppercorns slightly.

3 Layer mushrooms, garlic slices, and peppercorns in a glass bowl.

4 Combine olive oil, champagne vinegar, and brandy and pour over mushroom combination. Cover tightly and marinate at room temperature.

5 Turn container approximately every hour for 6 to 8 hours. Do not marinate more than 8 hours or mushrooms will become mushy. Refrigerate after 6 hours.

6 Drain and serve chilled as hors d'oeuvres or first course.

STUFFED BAKED MUSHROOMS

YIELD: SERVES 4 AS ENTRÉE, 6–8 AS HORS D'OEUVRES

16 *large mushrooms*
2 *large shallots*
1 *tablespoon extra virgin olive oil*
2 *cloves garlic*
$1/3$ *cup toasted pine nuts*
$1/2$ *teaspoon nutmeg*

1 *teaspoon Tabasco sauce*
2 *tablespoons Worcestershire sauce*
1 *egg, beaten*
1 *cup grated Havarti cheese*
3 *tablespoons unsalted margarine or butter, softened*

1 Preheat oven to 400°.

2 Wipe mushrooms clean and remove stems. Set caps aside and finely chop stems. Finely chop shallots.

3 Heat olive oil over low heat and add shallots. Cook 1 minute, stirring constantly, and add chopped mushroom stems. Cook 1 more minute. Remove from heat and set aside to cool.

4 Mash and mince garlic cloves and combine with toasted pine nuts, nutmeg, Tabasco sauce, Worcestershire sauce, and beaten egg.

5 Grate Havarti cheese and add to stuffing mixture. Stir in cooled sautéed mushrooms and shallots, and blend well.

6 Rub mushroom caps inside and out with softened margarine or butter, and place in shallow baking dish.

7 Mound stuffing into each mushroom cap, and pack with fingers or the back of a spoon.

8 Bake uncovered in 400° oven 10 to 15 minutes, depending on size of mushroom caps. Serve immediately as hors d'oeuvres, first course, or entrée.

Variation
Three-fourths cup cooked ham, shrimp, crabmeat, or lobster may be substituted for grated cheese. A little lemon juice complements a seafood stuffing.

DEVILED EGGS

YIELD: 24 STUFFED EGG HALVES

12 eggs
1 dill pickle, minced
3 green onions, minced
½ cup mayonnaise

2 tablespoons Dijon mustard
salt and pepper
paprika or parsley for garnish

1 Hard-boil eggs (see *Eggs*), and peel when they are cool. Cut eggs in half lengthwise, being careful not to break the whites. Scoop out yolks and put them in a bowl.
2 Mash yolks with a fork, then add dill pickle, green onions, mayon-naise, Dijon mustard, salt, and pepper. Blend until smooth.
3 Carefully spoon yolk filling into white halves. Decorate with paprika or parsley. Garnish with radish flowers and lemon crowns.

★

JICAMA MEXICANA

A south-of-the-border favorite increasingly popular with los americanos norteños. *Serve with Mexican food or as a cool snack anytime.*

YIELD: SERVES 6–8 AS APPETIZER

1 small jicama root
1 tablespoon chili powder
2 limes

1 Wash and peel well-chilled jicama; slice into small sticks about ½ inch wide.
2 Put chili powder into a small wide dish and place on a serving tray with jicama sticks.
3 Slice limes into wedges and arrange on platter with jicama.
4 To eat, squeeze lime over jicama and dip into chili powder.

★

CELERY

Some recommendations for serving celery as an appetizer or first course:

Fresh Celery Hearts
Clean celery (see *Celery*). Remove the tender heart and serve simply on ice. Leave small leaves intact for appearance; they can be tasty when young. Accompany fresh celery hearts

with good olives and freshly shelled nuts. Serve with champagne, dry sherry, or fresh fruit juice.

Stuffed Celery

Clean and string celery and cut into 4-inch sections. Fill with Jalapeño Pimiento Cheese (page 137) or other favorite concoctions.

Chip and Dip Alternative

Use celery stalks and other raw or blanched vegetables instead of chips. Especially delicious with creamy dips. Celery and other vegetables are a delight with spicy salsas as well.

WALDORF COCKTAIL

A nutritious nonalcoholic beginning.

YIELD: 1 SERVING

*2 cups freshly extracted celery and
  apple juice combined*

*several tender stalks of celery
whole walnut halves*

1 Chill juice (allow 2 cups per person).
2 Serve with stalks of celery and walnut halves arranged colorfully on a platter.

TEXAS CAVIAR

A fun dish for New Year's parties.

YIELD: 12–16 SERVINGS

*1 pound dried black-eyed peas,
  cooked and seasoned (see Basic
  Beans, page 121)*
toast points or crackers

*unsalted margarine or butter
finely chopped purple onion
1 or more Mexican salsas (pages
  54–56)*

1 Serve cooked, seasoned black-eyed peas at room temperature in a large bowl or serving dish.
2 Arrange breads, margarine or butter, and other condiments in containers around the black-eyed peas.
3 Encourage your guests to serve themselves in classical caviar style.

★

MOTHER'S CHEESE PUFFS

YIELD: 48 PUFFS

48 pimiento-stuffed olives
2 cups grated natural sharp cheese
½ cup cold unsalted margarine or
*   butter*

1 cup sifted unbleached white flour
½ teaspoon paprika

1 Drain olives and set aside.
2 Grate cheese and cold margarine or butter. Allow to warm and soften.
3 Blend cheese with margarine or butter. Stir in flour and paprika; mix well.
4 Wrap 1 teaspoon cheese mixture around each olive, covering it completely.
5 Arrange covered olives on baking sheet and freeze until firm. (Transfer to plastic bag or other covered container if puffs are not to be baked immediately.) Keep frozen until baking time.
6 Bake 15 minutes in preheated 400° oven on ungreased baking sheet and serve hot.

★

BABA-GHANNOUJ

Diane Roberts

YIELD: 2½ CUPS

2 medium eggplants
2 cloves garlic
2 tablespoons tahini (sesame butter)
juice of 1 lemon

⅛ teaspoon cayenne pepper
¼ teaspoon tamari soy sauce
yogurt for garnish
parsley for garnish

1 Preheat oven to 450°.
2 Wash eggplants, split into halves, and make 3 or 4 lengthwise slits in the interior of each half (being sure not to cut through the skin). Place cut side down on an oiled baking sheet.
3 Bake undisturbed for 1 hour until skin is crispy (almost charred). This gives a smoky flavor.
4 Puree all ingredients except yogurt and parsley in a food processor or blender. (Chop eggplant into smaller pieces if necessary before pureeing.)
5 Cool and serve garnished with a dollop of yogurt and a sprig of parsley. Traditionally scooped up with pita bread.

★

AVOCADO CHILE DIP

Nita Graves

YIELD: ABOUT 3½ CUPS

12 green chiles
3 ripe avocados
3 tablespoons low-fat milk
3 tablespoons Vinaigrette Dressing
  (page 93)
16 ounces ricotta cheese, room
  temperature

2 cloves garlic, mashed and minced
¼ teaspoon tamari soy sauce (the
  liquid soy sauce blends more
  evenly than salt)

1 Roast and peel green chiles (see
  Chile Peppers).
2 Peel, seed, and mash avocados and
  combine with chopped chiles.
3 Add milk, vinaigrette dressing, soft-

ened ricotta cheese, minced garlic,
and tamari soy sauce.
4 Blend to creamy consistency and
  serve as a dip.

★

TOFU DILL DIP

YIELD: ABOUT 1½ CUPS

½ cup low-fat yogurt
½ cup low-fat, low-sodium cottage
  cheese
4 ounces tofu

2 teaspoons tamari soy sauce
2 teaspoons white pepper
2 teaspoons dill weed

1 In a blender, thoroughly blend
  yogurt, cottage cheese, and tofu.
2 Season with tamari soy sauce, white

pepper, and dill weed. Blend and
serve.

★

SAN FRANCISCO VEGETABLE PÂTÉ

*My version of the dish created by Chef Jacky Robert at Ernie's Restaurant in
San Francisco, California.*

YIELD: 24 SERVINGS

28 tomatoes
2 purple onions
6 garlic cloves

¼ cup oil
½ pound broccoli
½ head cauliflower

2 carrots
1 medium turnip
2–3 green beans
½ teaspoon white pepper
salt (optional)
1 pound cream cheese, room
   temperature

1 pound unsalted margarine or
   butter, room temperature
4 packages unflavored gelatin
1½ cups dry white wine
4 egg whites

1 Peel, seed, and juice tomatoes. Chop onions and garlic.
2 Sauté tomatoes, onions, and garlic in oil for 1 hour. Set aside to cool.
3 Cut broccoli and cauliflower into florets, carrots into long rounds, and turnip into square- or tri-angular-shaped sticks. Leave green beans whole.
4 Blanch vegetables by immersing in boiling water until tender.
5 In a food processor, combine white pepper, salt, cream cheese, and margarine or butter.
6 When tomato mixture has cooled, combine it with cheese mixture in food processor.

7 Soften and dissolve gelatin in dry white wine and bring mixture to simmer. Remove from heat and cool to room temperature.
8 Combine gelatin mixture with tomato-cheese mixture.
9 Whip egg whites and fold in.
10 Spread tomato-cheese-gelatin mixture in a lightly oiled terrine mold between layers of broccoli, cauliflower, carrots, green beans, and turnip.
11 Chill overnight and carefully unmold. Garnish with parsley and serve.

2

STOCKS AND SAUCES

STOCKS

★

COURT BOUILLON

This is a light, quick, aromatic broth used for poaching or steaming seafood, or, with the fish parts omitted, a vegetable broth used to cook and flavor vegetables.

YIELD: 1½ – 2 QUARTS

1 medium white onion
1 stalk celery
2 shallots or green onions
6 parsley stems
1 pound fish bones, heads, and other trimmings
2 quarts cold water

½ cup dry white wine
3 tablespoons champagne vinegar
6 white peppercorns
6 black peppercorns
1 bay leaf
½ teaspoon thyme
½ teaspoon fennel seed

1 Coarsely chop onion, celery, and shallots or green onions.
2 Remove parsley leaves from the stems. Reserve leaves for another use, as they darken the bouillon.
3 Combine chopped vegetables and parsley stems with all other ingre-

dients in a 4-quart saucepan or stockpot. (Omit fish parts if making vegetable bouillon.)
4 Bring to simmer and cook uncovered 30 minutes.
5 Strain through a cheesecloth-lined sieve and cool.

★

VEGETABLE STOCK

YIELD: ABOUT 3 QUARTS

3 medium leeks
4 stalks celery
4 carrots
2 purple onions
3 green onions
3 cloves garlic
2 medium tomatoes
1 large bell pepper

2 tablespoons extra virgin olive oil
1 cup dry white wine
6 white peppercorns
6 black peppercorns
3 whole cloves
2 bay leaves
½ teaspoon thyme
4 quarts water

1 Wash and coarsely chop leeks, celery, carrots, purple onions, green onions, garlic, tomatoes, and bell pepper.
2 Heat olive oil in a large stockpot and add chopped vegetables.
3 Cook over medium heat 15 minutes, stirring often.
4 Add white wine and cook about 3 more minutes.
5 Add white peppercorns, black pep-

percorns, cloves, bay leaves, thyme, and water to stockpot.
6 Bring to boil and reduce to simmer. Cook 2 hours, occasionally skimming off any material that may rise to the top.
7 Remove from heat and strain through a cheesecloth-lined sieve. Cool uncovered and refrigerate or freeze until needed.

★

WHITE STOCK
YIELD: 3 – 4 QUARTS

1 medium purple onion
3 medium carrots
3 medium leeks
1 shallot
4 green onions
3½ pounds chicken backs, necks, bones, and other pieces

3 pounds veal bones
1 teaspoon white wine vinegar
6 white peppercorns
½ teaspoon thyme
3 parsley stems (leaves removed)
1 bay leaf

1 Wash and coarsely chop purple onion, carrots, leeks, shallot, and green onions.
2 Place prepared vegetables, chicken pieces, and veal bones into a large stockpot.
3 Add enough water to cover by 1 inch.
4 Add white wine vinegar, white peppercorns, thyme, parsley stems, and bay leaf.

5 Bring to boil and reduce to simmer. Cook 2 hours, occasionally skimming off material that rises to the top.
6 Remove from heat and strain through a cheesecloth-lined sieve. Cool uncovered to room temperature and refrigerate for a few hours.
7 Remove from refrigerator and skim off fat. Stock may be used as is or further reduced.

★

BROWN POULTRY STOCK
YIELD: 3 – 4 QUARTS

1 bunch leeks
4 stalks celery

3 carrots
1 purple onion

6 pounds poultry pieces and bones,
  cooked or uncooked
6 whole peppercorns
4 whole cloves

3 bay leaves
½ teaspoon thyme
1 cup white wine

1 Preheat oven to 500°.
2 Wash and coarsely chop leeks, celery, carrots, and purple onion.
3 Arrange these vegetables with the meat and bones in a large roasting pan.
4 Roast at 500° until bones and vegetables are nicely browned (approximately 1 hour), turning occasionally.
5 Remove from oven and place meat, bones, and vegetables in a large stockpot.
6 Add enough room-temperature water to cover ingredients by 1 inch.
7 Add peppercorns, cloves, bay leaves, and thyme.
8 Bring to boil and reduce to simmer.
9 Pour fat out of roasting pan.
10 Deglaze pan by setting it over a low flame on top of the stove.

11 Add white wine to roasting pan and reduce to ½ cup, stirring constantly and scraping the bottom of the pan.
12 Add the deglazing liquid to the simmering stock.
13 From time to time, skim off fat and other material that floats to the top.
14 When meat is falling apart, strain all solid ingredients out of the stock.
15 Filter stock through several layers of cheesecloth and allow to cool, skimming off fat.
16 The stock is now ready to be used as a base for soups or sauces. It may be reduced further for easy storage.

★

FISH STOCK
YIELD: ABOUT 3 QUARTS

1 shallot
3 large purple onions
2 carrots
2 leeks
2 stalks celery
8–10 parsley stems
3 tablespoons extra virgin olive oil
1 cup dry white wine
3½ pounds fresh scrap pieces of fish
  or fish bones

1 bay leaf
1 teaspoon thyme
juice of ½ lemon
6 white peppercorns
3 whole cloves
3 whole allspice
½ teaspoon crushed red pepper
4 quarts water

1 Clean and coarsely chop shallot, purple onions, carrots, leeks, and celery.

2 Remove parsley leaves from washed parsley stems. Reserve leaves for other purposes because they will darken the stock.

3 Heat olive oil in a large stockpot over medium heat. Stir in vegetables and cook 15 minutes.

4 Pour in dry white wine and deglaze the pot.

5 Add pieces of fish and fish bones.

6 Add bay leaf, thyme, lemon juice, white peppercorns, cloves, allspice, red pepper, and water.

7 Bring stock to low simmer and cook 40 minutes. Remove from heat and cool enough for easy handling.

8 Filter stock through a cheesecloth-lined sieve.

9 Stock can now be further reduced or used as is in a variety of recipes.

★

LOBSTER FUMET (STOCK)

YIELD: 4 QUARTS

2 tablespoons extra virgin olive oil
8–10 cups broken lobster shells and other leftover pieces
2 medium carrots
1 leek
1 medium purple onion
2 stalks celery
2 shallots
2 medium tomatoes

¼ cup brandy
1 bay leaf
3 whole cloves
6 white peppercorns
6 black peppercorns
1 cup dry white wine
5 quarts water (preferably bottled or spring water)

1 In a large, deep skillet, heat olive oil over medium-high heat. Break lobster shells and other scraps into small pieces and add to skillet. Cook 10 minutes, stirring often.

2 Slice carrots and chop leek, purple onion, and celery. Coarsely chop shallots and tomatoes. Combine prepared vegetables and set aside.

3 Add brandy to skillet and swirl it around with the shell pieces over high heat.

4 Tilt pan slightly to ignite brandy with gas flame, or light with match. Proceed with caution. Shake pan a bit to keep contents moving and burning evenly until flame burns out.

5 When flames have subsided, add prepared vegetables and stir well. Cook another 10 minutes, stirring often.

6 Add bay leaf, cloves, and peppercorns to cooking mixture.

7 Blend in seasonings and add dry white wine. Cook 2 or 3 minutes.

8 Transfer to a large stockpot. Add water and bring to boil, then simmer for 30 minutes.

9 Remove from stove and strain.

10 Use stock as is or reduce for flavor intensification and/or convenience in storage. The stock will keep for months in the freezer.

BUTTERS AND BUTTER SAUCES

★

BEURRE BLANC

A rich, smooth treat from France that has a practical versatility. Serve with poached seafoods, cooked vegetables, or egg dishes.

YIELD: ABOUT 1 CUP

1 shallot or 1 tablespoon minced
  green onion
¼ teaspoon white pepper

¼ cup champagne vinegar
¼ cup dry white wine
1 cup unsalted margarine or butter

1 Finely mince shallot or green onion and combine with white pepper, champagne vinegar, and white wine.
2 Place in a medium-sized non-aluminum saucepan and simmer until mixture has reduced to about 2 tablespoons.
3 Meanwhile, cut margarine or butter into 1-tablespoon pieces.
4 When reduction is ready, remove from heat and beat in butter pats, 1 or 2 at a time. Take care to beat each addition thoroughly before adding more.
5 When 1 stick of butter has been incorporated into sauce, place pan over low heat for 1 to 2 minutes and continue to whip in the butter pats. Work quickly, do not overheat, and the sauce should not separate. If necessary, remove from heat to finish adding butter. Sauce should be thick and creamy.
6 Serve immediately or hold in a warm place until serving time.

★

HOT LEMON-LIME BUTTER

YIELD: 2 CUPS

1 cup unsalted margarine or butter,
  or combination

juice of 4 lemons
juice of 4 limes

1 Soften margarine and/or butter and set aside. Heat lemon and lime juice and remove from heat.
2 Drop by small bits into the juice and whip until all of it is incorpo-rated. Consistency should be creamy, rather than oily.
3 Serve immediately with fish or vegetables.

★

ANCHOVY BUTTER

YIELD: ABOUT 1 CUP

2 shallots
1 clove garlic
½ can (1 tablespoon) anchovy fillets

1 cup unsalted margarine or butter,
or combination

1 Finely mince shallots and garlic.
2 Add to drained anchovy fillets.
3 Whip with margarine or butter.

4 Arrange decoratively in a bowl and chill 30 minutes. Serve with salmon steaks or beef.

★

FRESH HERB BUTTER

Herb butter can be made from a single herb or a combination of two or more. It is especially good served with poultry, meat, seafood, pasta, or fresh vegetables.

YIELD: ABOUT 1½ CUPS

juice of ½ lemon
2 shallots
1 cup fresh herb leaves (parsley,

basil, thyme, oregano, dill weed,
etc.) or ⅓ cup dried herbs
1 cup unsalted margarine or butter

1 Juice lemon, mince shallots, and wash and chop fresh herbs. Bring margarine or butter to room temperature.
2 In a food processor or by hand, blend all ingredients except butter.

3 Add butter, ½ stick at a time, and blend thoroughly.
4 Serve separately as a sauce or heated with fresh vegetables. Garnish your dish imaginatively with a few sprigs of fresh herbs.

★

GINGER-LIME BUTTER

Ann Clark, La Bonne Cuisine School
YIELD: ABOUT 1 CUP

2 tablespoons finely grated lime peel
6 ounces ginger, peeled and minced
8 shallots, chopped

2 tablespoons lime juice
1 cup unsalted butter

1 Puree all ingredients except butter in food processor or blender.
2 Add butter and puree until thoroughly blended.

3 Serve in a decorative manner as a condiment for fish, roast beef, or pasta.

★

PROVENÇALE BUTTER

Can be stored in the freezer indefinitely.

YIELD: ABOUT 2½ CUPS

2 cups unsalted margarine or butter
3 shallots or 4 green onions
12 cloves garlic
leaves from 1 bunch parsley

3 tablespoons dry white wine
juice of 1 lemon
½ teaspoon white pepper
¼ teaspoon nutmeg

1 Soften margarine or butter and set aside.
2 Coarsely chop shallots or onions, garlic, and parsley leaves.

3 Place all ingredients in a food processor or blender and blend until liquid is absorbed.

HOT EMULSIFIED SAUCES

★

HOLLANDAISE SAUCE

Do not use an aluminum pan for this recipe.

YIELD: 4–6 SERVINGS

3 egg yolks
juice of 1 lemon
½ cup unsalted margarine

½ cup unsalted butter
pinch of nutmeg
pinch of cayenne pepper

1 Separate eggs and place yolks in a round stainless steel bowl. Reserve whites for another purpose.
2 Add lemon juice to egg yolks and mix thoroughly. Set aside.
3 Over a low flame, melt together margarine and butter.
4 Select a pan large enough to hold the stainless steel bowl and fill it with an inch or so of water, creating a double-boiler effect.
5 Bring water in pan to simmer and place bowl of egg yolks in it, rotating bowl quickly and whipping yolks briskly with a whisk (figure 12a).
6 Very slowly at first, dribble in a few drops of the hot butter and margarine mixture, whipping constantly. As the sauce emulsifies, continue to add remaining butter, a little at a time (figure 12b), until all of it has been used and the sauce has thickened. The stainless steel bowl may have to be removed and then returned to the heat several times while the butter and margarine mixture is being added.
7 Add pinches of cayenne pepper and

nutmeg and set aside ready for use. If necessary, the hollandaise may be thinned by beating in a little warm water.

Caper Hollandaise
Stir 3 tablespoons well-drained capers into finished hollandaise. Serve with seafood and vegetables.

Curried Hollandaise
Add 1 tablespoon hot curry powder to sauce along with cayenne pepper and nutmeg. A surprising complement to omelets, frittatas, and soufflés.

Lime Hollandaise
Substitute the juice of 2 or 3 limes for lemon juice.

Mustard Hollandaise
Add 2 tablespoons Dijon mustard along with cayenne pepper and nutmeg.

Figure 12a

Figure 12b

Orange Hollandaise (Sauce Maltaise)

Substitute juice of 1 orange for the lemon juice. Also add 1 tablespoon finely grated orange rind along with cayenne pepper and nutmeg.

Restoring Broken Hollandaise

1 Whip 2 egg yolks in a round-bottomed metal bowl and warm slightly in pan or skillet with a little simmering water in it.

2 Dribble broken hollandaise into egg yolks, whisking briskly. Take care not to scramble the eggs.

3 Remove bowl from heat from time to time, if necessary. All of the sauce should be reemulsified.

★

BLENDER HOLLANDAISE

Variations and method of restoring are the same as for the preceding recipe.

YIELD: 4 – 6 SERVINGS

3 egg yolks
juice of 1 lemon
½ cup unsalted margarine

½ cup unsalted butter
pinch of nutmeg
pinch of cayenne pepper

1 Separate eggs and place yolks in a blender or food processor. Reserve whites for another purpose.

2 Add lemon juice to egg yolks and blend thoroughly for 2 minutes.

3 Over a low flame, melt together margarine and butter.

4 Turn on blender and, very slowly at first, dribble in a few drops of hot margarine and butter. As the mix-

ture begins to emulsify, add the remaining butter and margarine in an increasing steady stream until all of it has been used and the sauce has thickened.

5 Add pinches of cayenne pepper and nutmeg. If necessary, the hollandaise sauce may be thinned by blending in a little warm water.

★

BÉARNAISE SAUCE

Do not use an aluminum pan for this recipe.

YIELD: 4–6 SERVINGS

2 tablespoons chopped shallots or
green onions
½ cup tarragon vinegar
½ cup dry white wine
2 tablespoons chervil or parsley
2 tablespoons tarragon

3 egg yolks
½ cup unsalted margarine
½ cup unsalted butter
pinch of cayenne pepper
pinch of nutmeg
pinch of white pepper

1 Chop shallots or green onions, and combine with vinegar, wine, chervil or parsley, and tarragon.
2 Bring to simmer in a small saucepan and reduce liquid to a little less than ⅓ cup.
3 Remove saucepan from heat and allow to cool.
4 Separate eggs and place yolks in a round stainless steel bowl. Reserve whites for another purpose.
5 Strain cooked herbs from saucepan, reserving herbs, and add liquid to egg yolks and whisk well.
6 Over low heat, melt together margarine and butter.
7 Select a pan several inches wider in diameter than the bowl with the egg yolks in it so that the bowl can spin freely. Fill pan with an inch or so of water and bring the water to a gentle simmer. Do not boil.
8 Place bowl of egg yolks and reduc-

tion liquid into pan of simmering water, rotating bowl quickly and whipping yolks briskly with a wire whisk.
9 Very slowly at first, dribble in a few drops of the hot butter and margarine mixture, whipping constantly. As the sauce emulsifies, continue to add the remaining butter and margarine, a little at a time, until all of it has been used and the sauce has thickened. The stainless steel bowl may have to be removed and then returned to the heat several times while the butter and margarine is being added to maintain the proper consistency.
10 Add 1 tablespoon of the reserved cooked herbs and pinches of cayenne pepper and nutmeg. If necessary, the sauce may be thinned by beating in a little warm water.

Tomato Béarnaise (Sauce Choron)
Instead of step 10 in béarnaise recipe, beat 6 tablespoons of tomato paste and a pinch of cayenne pepper into the sauce.

Mint Béarnaise (Sauce Paloise)
Substitute 4 tablespoons chopped fresh mint for the chervil or parsley and tarragon. Also add 1 teaspoon white crème de menthe to reduction as it cools in step 3. Excellent with lamb.

WHITE SAUCES

★

CREAM GRAVY

YIELD: 3¼ CUPS

*3 tablespoons drippings from frying
   meat or chicken*
*3 tablespoons unbleached white
   flour*

3 cups milk
½ teaspoon cayenne pepper
pinch of salt

1 Pour out all but 3 tablespoons of
   drippings from the cooking pan.
   Prepare a roux by stirring in 3 tablespoons flour. (Seasoned flour left
   over from dredging meat may be
   used.) Cook mixture over low heat,
   stirring until golden brown.
2 Meanwhile, heat milk to simmer.

3 Remove pan from heat and whisk
   hot milk into roux. Return pan to
   medium-low heat and stir until
   gravy reaches desired consistency.
   Season with cayenne pepper and
   salt, if desired, and serve
   immediately.

★

BÉCHAMEL SAUCE

YIELD: 3 CUPS

3 cups low-fat milk
*2 tablespoons unsalted margarine
   or butter*
*2 tablespoons unbleached white
   flour*

salt to taste (optional)
white pepper to taste
Tabasco sauce to taste
pinch of nutmeg

1 Pour milk into a saucepan and bring
   to a simmer while preparing roux.
2 Melt margarine or butter in skillet
   or sauté pan until it starts to foam.
   Stir in flour to make roux and continue stirring over low heat until
   roux turns golden.

3 Pour milk slowly into roux, blending with whisk all the time.
4 When sauce has reached desired
   consistency, add seasonings to taste.
5 If sauce is not to be served immediately, remove from heat and cover
   with waxed paper or plastic wrap.

Velouté Sauce
Substitute unsalted chicken stock for
milk in Béchamel Sauce recipe.

★

TOFU BÉCHAMEL
YIELD: ABOUT 3½ CUPS

8 ounces tofu
¼ teaspoon white pepper
¼ teaspoon garlic powder
1 teaspoon fructose
1 cup water
2 tablespoons unsalted margarine
 or butter

2 tablespoons unbleached white
 flour
½ teaspoon black pepper
¼ teaspoon nutmeg
2–3 dashes of Tabasco sauce

1 Place tofu in a blender with white pepper, garlic powder, and fructose. Blend well.
2 Mix 2 cups of this blend with 1 cup water and heat in a saucepan over low flame.
3 While tofu mixture is heating, melt margarine or butter in another pan until it starts to foam. Then stir in flour to make a roux. Stir over low heat until it turns golden (not brown).
4 The tofu mixture should be sim-mering as the roux turns golden. Turn off heat under both and pour the tofu mixture slowly into the roux, whipping with a whisk all the time.
5 When thoroughly blended, season with black pepper (or white pepper, if the desired color of the ulti-mate dish requires it) and nutmeg. Add Tabasco sauce.
6 If sauce is not to be served imme-diately, remove from heat and cover with waxed paper or plastic wrap.

Tofu Mornay
After step 5 of Tofu Béchamel recipe, return mixture to low flame. Stirring continuously, slowly add 1 to 1½ cups grated cheese, depending on de-sired consistency. Stir until cheese is melted.

T O M A T O   S A U C E S

★

T O M A T O   A N D   L E E K   S A U C E

Y I E L D :   6   S E R V I N G S

12 large ripe tomatoes (7 cups finely chopped)
2 large stalks celery (²/₃ cup chopped)
6 cloves garlic
2 medium leeks (2 cups chopped)
2 tablespoons extra virgin olive oil
2 bay leaves

¹/₂ teaspoon thyme
¹/₂ teaspoon chervil
¹/₂ teaspoon cayenne pepper
¹/₄ teaspoon oregano
¹/₈ teaspoon raw turbinado sugar
1 cup dry red wine
¹/₂ cup chicken or vegetable stock

1 Peel, juice, and seed tomatoes (see *Tomatoes*). Finely chop by hand or puree in food processor. Set aside.
2 Remove strings from celery and chop. Mash and mince garlic. Chop leeks and wash (see *Leeks*).
3 Heat olive oil in large skillet and add garlic and leeks. Cook 3 or 4 minutes, stirring frequently.

4 Add celery. Cook 5 more minutes.
5 Add tomatoes, bay leaves, thyme, chervil, cayenne pepper, oregano, and sugar. Cook 1 hour, stirring occasionally.
6 Add wine and chicken or vegetable stock. Cook 30 minutes and serve with pastas or as a sauce with shrimp, chicken, or veal.

★

S E A F O O D   C O C K T A I L   S A U C E

Y I E L D :   3   C U P S

1 cup chili sauce
¹/₂ cup ketchup
3 tablespoons horseradish
1 tablespoon Worcestershire sauce

juice of 1 lemon
dash of Tabasco sauce
freshly ground black pepper to taste

Mix together all ingredients and serve with boiled shrimp, crab, or any other seafood.

★

POP LOWERY'S BARBECUE SAUCE

YIELD: ABOUT 4 CUPS

*grated and chopped peel and juice of
  1 lemon*
12 ounces chili sauce
14 ounces ketchup
2 tablespoons Worcestershire sauce
2 tablespoons brown sugar

4 tablespoons prepared mustard
2 teaspoons black pepper
1 teaspoon chili powder
1 teaspoon garlic powder
½ teaspoon Tabasco sauce
¼ cup extra virgin olive oil

1 Mix all ingredients together and simmer about 20 minutes over low heat.

2 Use to baste meats or poultry while grilling over charcoal.

3 Reheat remaining sauce and serve warm at the table.

MEXICAN SALSAS AND SAUCES

★

SALSA PICANTE

Pamela Navarez

YIELD: ABOUT 1 QUART

1 28-ounce can tomatoes
1 7-ounce can pickled jalapeños
3 serrano peppers

1 small white onion
2 cloves garlic

1 Remove stems from jalapeños. Peel and chop onion.
2 Place all ingredients in a blender or food processor and blend thoroughly.

★

SALSA FRESCA

Pamela Navarez

YIELD: ABOUT 1 QUART

4 large ripe tomatoes
1 large white onion

8 serrano peppers
1 small bunch cilantro

1 Dice tomatoes and onion.
2 Mince peppers and coarsely chop cilantro.
3 Toss together.

★

WESTLAKE SALSA FRESCA

YIELD: 1½ QUARTS

3 dozen serrano peppers
4 ripe tomatoes
8–12 tomatillos
6 cloves garlic
1 large purple onion
3 tablespoons chopped cilantro

1 teaspoon cracked black peppercorns
¼ teaspoon salt
1 tablespoon extra virgin olive oil
⅓ cup cilantro vinegar (see Herb-Flavored Vinegar, page 98)

1 Dry-roast serrano peppers in a cast-iron skillet (see *Chile Peppers*).
2 While peppers are roasting, peel, core, seed, juice, and chop tomatoes, and place in a large mixing bowl.
3 Remove outer skin from tomatillos and parboil for 60 seconds. When cool, chop coarsely and add to chopped tomatoes.
4 Coarsely chop roasted peppers and add to mixing bowl.
5 Mash and mince garlic, coarsely chop purple onion, and finely chop cilantro. Add to mixing bowl.
6 Stir in black pepper, salt, olive oil, and cilantro vinegar.
7 Stir salsa until well blended and serve immediately with tortilla chips or store in covered container in the refrigerator. Salsa fresca is best served immediately.

★

SALSA VERDE

Pamela Navarez

YIELD: ABOUT 1 QUART

1½ pounds tomatillos
½ white onion
4 serrano peppers
3 cloves garlic

½ bunch cilantro
¾ teaspoon oregano
dash black pepper

1 Peel tomatillos and wash thoroughly.
2 Cover tomatillos with water in a large saucepan and simmer until just tender, about 3 or 4 minutes. Allow to cool about 20 minutes.
3 Place everything in a blender and blend until smooth, adding some cooking liquid if necessary. If using a food processor, process onion, peppers, garlic, and cilantro thoroughly. Then add tomatillos and seasonings and process again.

★

SALSA CHIPOTLE

Pamela Navarez

YIELD: ABOUT 1 QUART

1 7-ounce can chipotle peppers
1 28-ounce can tomatoes (Progresso whole, peeled tomatoes with basil)

1 small white onion, quartered
1 tablespoon vinegar (optional)

1 Wearing rubber gloves, seed and stem the chipotle peppers.
2 Add all ingredients, including liquid from peppers, to blender and puree well.

★

CHILE PETÍN SAUCE

Lillian Boehm

YIELD: ABOUT 5 CUPS

3 medium onions (4 cups chopped)
8 cloves garlic
1 cup tiny red chile petín peppers

1 teaspoon salt
½ cup white wine vinegar

1 Chop onions and garlic.
2 Combine with chile petín peppers and coarsely chop in a food processor.
3 Place mixture in a bowl and allow to age (unrefrigerated) for 3 days.
After 3 days, stir in salt and pour vinegar on top of sauce.
4 Set aside and age 8 more days. After aging, place in glass jars and refrigerate. (The jars do not have to be sealed.)

MARINADE

★

SHISH KEBAB MARINADE

An all-purpose marinade for vegetables, meats, and fish. Leftover marinade can be heated and thickened with arrowroot to be used as a sauce.

YIELD: ABOUT 3 CUPS

1 purple onion
4 cloves garlic
1 cup sherry
1 cup water
2 tablespoons tamari soy sauce
2 tablespoons Worcestershire sauce

3 tablespoons freshly grated ginger
3 bay leaves
½ teaspoon cayenne pepper
½ teaspoon coarsely ground black pepper
juice of 1 lemon

1 Slice onion very thinly and mash and mince garlic. Combine onion and garlic with all other ingredients.
2 Cube and skewer vegetables, meat, and seafood, or any combination thereof, and marinate in the prepared mixture 2 to 3 hours.
3 Remove from the marinade and grill (see *Grilling*).

3

SOUPS

CREAMS AND PUREES

★

CREAMY WATERCRESS SOUP
YIELD: 6 SERVINGS

8 cups chicken stock
4 bunches fresh watercress
2 cups buttermilk
½ teaspoon prepared horseradish

white pepper and salt to taste
½ cup yogurt
paprika (optional)

1 Heat chicken stock to simmering. Meanwhile, chop watercress.
2 Add chopped watercress to stock, simmer 30 minutes, and cool.
3 Puree in food processor with buttermilk, horseradish, and white pepper and salt to taste.

4 Chill 3 to 4 hours, if possible. Soup will be thin and delicate.
5 Serve in chilled bowls (preferably on ice) and garnish with a dollop of yogurt sprinkled with paprika or topped with a fresh watercress leaf.

★

CREAMY CAULIFLOWER SOUP WITH CORN AND RICE
YIELD: 6–8 SERVINGS

1 large cauliflower
3 onions
2 medium potatoes
4 cloves garlic
4 tablespoons olive oil
2 cups white wine
8 cups chicken or vegetable stock
1 tablespoon Worcestershire sauce
1 teaspoon thyme
½ teaspoon sage

1 teaspoon chervil
pinch of cayenne pepper
½ teaspoon black pepper
3 ears corn
¼ teaspoon cumin
3 bay leaves
2 cups cooked brown rice (see Basic Grains, page 121)
tamari soy sauce or salt to taste

1 Break cauliflower into flowerets, chop onions, peel and dice potatoes, and chop garlic.
2 Heat 3 tablespoons olive oil in a

large soup pot and add cauliflower, onion, garlic, and potatoes.
3 Cook over low heat, stirring frequently, until the vegetables begin

to soften. Add white wine and simmer another 4 to 5 minutes.

4 Add 7 cups of the stock, Worcestershire sauce, thyme, sage,
chervil, cayenne pepper, and black
pepper. Simmer until all ingredients
are completely soft.

5 While vegetables are simmering,
slice the fresh corn from the ears.

6 In a sauté pan or saucepan, heat the
remaining tablespoon of olive oil
over a low flame and add corn, stirring constantly for a few minutes.

Then add cumin, bay leaves, and
the remaining cup of stock, and
cook until corn is tender.

7 When cauliflower and other vegetables are thoroughly cooked, cool
soup and puree in a food processor.
Add a bit of water if mixture becomes too thick.

8 Return the soup to soup pan and
stir in the cooked corn (remove
bay leaves) and cooked brown rice.
Season with desired amount of tamari soy sauce or salt.

★

CREAMY BROCCOLI AND COUSCOUS SOUP

YIELD: 8 SERVINGS

3 medium leeks
5 cloves garlic
2 large bunches broccoli (about 8
   cups chopped)
3 tablespoons unsalted margarine
   or butter
½ teaspoon cayenne pepper
¼ teaspoon nutmeg

½ teaspoon dill weed
1 teaspoon thyme
½ teaspoon oregano
¼ teaspoon white pepper
¼ cup Madeira wine
10¾ cups chicken or vegetable stock
¾ cup couscous

1 Chop and wash leeks (see *Leeks*).
2 Peel, mash, and mince garlic.
3 Coarsely chop washed broccoli.
4 Melt margarine or butter in large
soup pan or Dutch oven and sauté
leeks and garlic 3 to 5 minutes.
5 Add chopped broccoli and cook 5
minutes more.
6 Add cayenne pepper, nutmeg, dill
weed, thyme, oregano, white pepper, and Madeira wine.
7 Stir vegetables, herbs, and seasonings for a couple of minutes and
add 8 cups stock. Simmer uncovered 1 hour.
8 While soup is cooking, heat ¾ cup
stock to boiling. Turn off heat. Add

couscous. Cover and let stand 10
minutes.
9 In a food processor or blender,
puree prepared couscous with remaining 2 cups stock.
10 When soup has cooked 1 hour, remove from heat, cool for a few
minutes, and stir in couscous
puree. Stir well to blend
thoroughly.
11 Puree 3 cups of soup mixture until smooth and return puree to
soup pot.
12 Heat soup until warm enough to
serve and ladle into warm soup
bowls.

★

POTATO-LEEK SOUP

YIELD: 8–10 SERVINGS

4 leeks
4 stalks celery
3 carrots
1 onion
2 shallots
4–5 cloves garlic
3 tablespoons olive oil
6–8 medium potatoes
1 teaspoon thyme

1 teaspoon oregano
1 teaspoon basil
½ teaspoon cayenne pepper
2 bay leaves
1 teaspoon Worcestershire sauce
4 cups chicken or vegetable stock
2 cups low-fat milk
salt and pepper to taste

1 Coarsely chop leeks, celery, carrots, onion, shallots, and garlic.
2 Heat olive oil in a large Dutch oven and cook chopped vegetables over low heat, stirring often.
3 In the meantime, chop scrubbed unpeeled potatoes into ¼-inch cubes. Add to vegetables along with thyme, oregano, basil, cayenne pepper, bay leaves, and Worcestershire sauce. Cook 5 to 10 minutes, stirring often.

4 Add stock. Continue cooking until potatoes and carrots are soft but not mushy.
5 Remove from heat and allow to cool somewhat.
6 Puree half of soup mixture with milk. Return to pan.
7 Taste for seasoning and add desired amounts of salt and pepper.
8 Return to simmer and serve in warmed soup bowls.

★

CREAMY SPLIT PEA SOUP

YIELD: 6–8 SERVINGS

2 cups split peas
8 cups water or chicken stock or
*   combination*
1 slice bacon
1 purple onion

2 shallots
4 cloves garlic
1 bay leaf
½ teaspoon thyme
dash of Tabasco sauce

1 Rinse split peas.
2 Put peas, water or stock, and bacon in a soup pot and bring to simmer.
3 Chop purple onion, shallots, and garlic and add to soup.

4 Season with bay leaf, thyme, and a healthy dash of Tabasco sauce.
5 Simmer 1 hour. Remove from heat and allow to cool slightly.
6 Remove bay leaf and bacon.

7 Puree mixture in food processor or blender until very whipped and creamy.

8 Reheat and serve in warmed soup bowls, garnished with a small pat of margarine or butter.

★

PUREED SPLIT PEA AND LENTIL SOUP WITH BARLEY AND MUSHROOMS
YIELD: 8 – 10 SERVINGS

Base
2 medium onions
2 carrots
4 cloves garlic
1 cup lentils
1 cup split peas
8 cups stock
2 bay leaves
1 teaspoon oregano
1 teaspoon thyme
½ teaspoon celery seed
several dashes of Tabasco sauce

Barley
2 cups barley
2 cubes unsalted vegetable bouillon

4 cups stock or water
½ teaspoon white pepper
1 tablespoon unsalted margarine or butter

Mushrooms
1 pound fresh mushrooms
juice of 1 lemon
2 tablespoons unsalted margarine or butter
1 teaspoon thyme
1 tablespoon Worcestershire sauce
¼ cup red wine

1 Chop onions, slice carrots, mince garlic, and mix in a large soup pan with other soup base ingredients.

2 Simmer over a moderate flame until split peas and lentils are completely soft (approximately 1 hour). Set aside to cool.

3 Place barley, vegetable bouillon cubes, 4 cups stock or water, white pepper, and 1 tablespoon margarine or butter in a large covered saucepan and cook until barley is tender.

4 Slice mushrooms and toss with lemon juice. Allow to sit 30 minutes.

5 Melt 2 tablespoons margarine or butter in a sauté pan and sauté mushrooms over low heat 3 to 4 minutes.

6 Add thyme, Worcestershire sauce, and red wine and cook until liquid has evaporated.

7 Puree the cooled soup base mixture, adding water as needed for a smooth consistency.

8 Pour back into large soup pan and add cooked barley and mushrooms. Season to taste with tamari soy sauce and black pepper. Reheat to serve.

★

HAPPY'S BORSCHT

YIELD: 8 – 10 SERVINGS

5 beets
4 large carrots
1 purple onion
3 shallots
½ head small purple cabbage
3 medium tomatoes
¼ cup chopped parsley
4 stalks celery
2 tablespoons unsalted margarine
  or butter
1 tablespoon extra virgin olive oil

juice of ½ lemon
¼ cup red wine vinegar
9 whole black peppercorns
3 whole allspice berries
3 whole cloves
2 bay leaves
cayenne pepper and salt if desired
10 – 12 cups of chicken or vegetable
  stock
yogurt for garnish

1 Wash, peel, and grate beets and carrots.
2 Peel and coarsely chop onion and shallots.
3 Remove core from cabbage and chop or grate coarsely.
4 Core tomatoes and chop coarsely.
5 Wash and chop parsley (see *Parsley*) and celery.
6 Melt margarine or butter with olive oil in a large Dutch oven that has a cover, and sauté onion and shallots over low heat until soft.
7 Add beets, carrots, cabbage, and celery. Sauté about 10 minutes. Stir in tomatoes and cook another 10 minutes.
8 Stir in parsley, lemon juice, red wine vinegar, peppercorns, allspice,

cloves, bay leaves, cayenne pepper, salt, and stock. Cover and continue cooking over moderate heat about 2 hours, stirring occasionally.
9 When soup is thoroughly cooked, remove from heat and allow to cool 15 to 30 minutes.
10 When soup is cool enough to handle, strain mixture through a large sieve.
11 When liquid has drained from strainer, discard vegetables and filter broth through another sieve lined with several layers of cheesecloth.
12 Return strained soup to simmer to serve hot or chill thoroughly to serve cold. Garnish each bowl with a dollop of yogurt.

★

CREAMY LEEK AND PEPPER SOUP

YIELD: 6 – 8 SERVINGS

1 bunch leeks (3 cups chopped)
2 cups chopped purple onion
6 stalks celery

2 large shallots
½ cup unsalted margarine or butter
6 medium new potatoes

*1 6-ounce can green chile peppers,
  drained*
8 cups chicken or vegetable stock
*½ teaspoon coarsely ground red
  pepper*

1 teaspoon ground kelp
¼ teaspoon nutmeg
4 teaspoons fructose
½ cup dry sherry
2 cups low-fat milk

1 Chop leeks (see *Leeks*), purple onion, and celery, and mince shallots.
2 Melt margarine or butter in large Dutch oven. Sauté leeks, onion, celery, and shallots.
3 Wash and coarsely chop unpeeled new potatoes and add to simmering vegetables. Cook 5 more minutes, stirring often.
4 Add green chiles, stock, red pepper, kelp, nutmeg, and fructose. Simmer covered over medium heat for 1 hour, stirring occasionally.
5 Remove from heat and allow to cool somewhat, then puree in blender or food processor with sherry and milk.
6 Return to Dutch oven and slowly bring to simmer.
7 Serve in warm soup bowls with a sprinkling of coarsely ground black pepper.

★

CARROT BISQUE
YIELD: 8 SERVINGS

6–8 cups sliced carrots
1½ cups chopped leeks
2 stalks celery
6 cloves garlic
¼ cup unsalted margarine or butter
¼ teaspoon white pepper
¼ teaspoon cayenne pepper

¼ teaspoon curry powder
¼ teaspoon nutmeg
1 teaspoon fructose
6 cups chicken or vegetable stock
4 cups water
1 cup white wine
3 cups low-fat milk

1 Slice carrots into ¼-inch rounds but do not peel. Chop and wash leeks (see *Leeks*), string and chop celery, and slice garlic.
2 Melt margarine or butter in Dutch oven, and sauté carrots, leeks, celery, and garlic for 5 minutes over medium heat, stirring often.
3 Add white pepper, cayenne pepper, curry powder, nutmeg, and fructose and cook 2 to 3 minutes longer.
4 Add chicken or vegetable stock, water, and white wine. Simmer covered 1 hour over low heat.
5 Remove from heat and allow to cool.
6 Puree in food processor or blender with 3 cups low-fat milk.
7 Slowly rewarm and serve in warmed soup bowls with a light sprinkling of nutmeg.

★

PUREED CORN SOUP WITH CHICKEN AND ASPARAGUS TIPS

YIELD: 6 SERVINGS

4 cloves garlic
3 cups (about 6 medium ears) fresh corn
9 cups vegetable or chicken stock
2 tablespoons unsalted margarine or butter
1 tablespoon flour
1 tablespoon coarsely ground red pepper

2 whole chicken breasts (about 1 pound)
1 tablespoon extra virgin olive oil
¾ cup asparagus tips
½ cup low-fat milk
1 tablespoon cornstarch
1 teaspoon tamari soy sauce
fresh cilantro leaves for garnish

1 Mash and mince garlic. Slice the corn from the ears.
2 Heat vegetable or chicken stock to a simmer.
3 Heat margarine or butter in a large soup pan, and add garlic and fresh corn together. Sauté over medium heat, stirring frequently, for 7 minutes. Do not let the corn stick to the pan.
4 Add flour and red pepper and continue stirring and cooking for 5 minutes.
5 Add simmering stock to corn and cook covered over medium-low heat 1½ hours.
6 While soup is cooking, skin and bone chicken breasts. Cut chicken into small cubes.
7 Heat olive oil in a sauté pan and add chicken cubes. Cook 4 minutes over medium heat.
8 Add asparagus tips and cook 4 or 5 minutes longer, until chicken is done, but do not allow asparagus to get mushy. Remove from heat and set aside.
9 When soup has cooked 1½ hours, remove from heat, uncover, and allow to cool 15 to 20 minutes.
10 Puree and strain and return to soup pan. Add chicken and asparagus and bring to simmer.
11 Combine milk, cornstarch, and tamari soy sauce and blend with your fingers. Pour into simmering soup and cook 10 more minutes, stirring frequently.
12 Serve in warmed bowls garnished with a few leaves of fresh cilantro.

★

PINTO BEAN SOUP

YIELD: 12 LARGE SERVINGS

6 cups pinto beans
1 purple onion

3 tablespoons unsalted margarine or butter

10 cups chicken stock
8 cups water
1 bay leaf
¼ teaspoon finely ground black
   pepper

1 teaspoon thyme
1 teaspoon cumin
2 cups low-fat milk

1 Soak pinto beans overnight in enough water to cover.
2 When ready to cook, chop purple onion. In a large cast-iron Dutch oven, melt margarine or butter and sauté onion until transparent.
3 Add chicken stock, water, bay leaf, black pepper, thyme, and cumin and cook covered 4 to 6 hours over medium heat.

4 Remove from heat and discard bay leaf.
5 Measure out 3 cups of the soup and puree with milk until smooth.
6 Stir puree back in with the rest of the soup and rewarm over low heat. Taste soup and adjust seasoning as needed.

★

LEEK AND ARTICHOKE SOUP

Pamela Navarez

YIELD: 8–10 SERVINGS

3–4 leeks
2 cloves garlic
3 tablespoons clarified butter
2 teaspoons tarragon
3 cans artichoke bottoms, drained

8 cups light chicken stock
1 teaspoon white pepper
¼ cup toasted, peeled, and finely
   chopped hazelnuts
chopped parsley for garnish

1 Chop and wash leeks (see *Leeks*). Mash and mince garlic.
2 Heat butter and add leeks. Sauté until limp.
3 Add garlic and tarragon and sauté 3 or 4 more minutes, stirring occasionally.

4 Add artichoke bottoms, chicken stock, and white pepper. Bring to a boil and simmer 5 minutes.
5 Puree in batches until smooth.
6 Garnish each serving with hazelnuts and chopped parsley.

VEGETABLE SOUPS

★

SPLIT PEA VEGETABLE SOUP
YIELD: 8–10 SERVINGS

1 cup dried split peas
8 cups chicken or vegetable stock
4 tablespoons unsalted margarine
or butter
6 new potatoes
4 medium carrots
2 large purple onions
3 stalks celery
3 ears corn

3 cloves garlic
3 cups stewed tomatoes (canned or
fresh)
½ teaspoon cayenne pepper (or to
taste)
3 bay leaves
1 teaspoon thyme
½ teaspoon tarragon

1 Simmer split peas in 2 cups stock and 1 tablespoon margarine or butter for 30 to 40 minutes.

2 While peas are cooking, prepare vegetables: Cube unpeeled potatoes. Slice unpeeled carrots into ¼-inch rounds. Chop onions into large pieces. Remove strings from celery and chop into ¼-inch pieces. Slice corn from cobs. Mash and mince garlic.

3 Melt 3 tablespoons margarine or butter in a pan large enough to hold entire soup.

4 Add potatoes and carrots, and cook over a low flame 10 minutes, stirring frequently.

5 Add onions, celery, and corn, and cook another 10 minutes. Continue to stir frequently.

6 Combine stewed tomatoes with remaining 6 cups of stock and add to the cooking vegetable mixture. Increase heat to high. Bring soup to simmer and reduce heat.

7 Add cayenne pepper, bay leaves, thyme, and tarragon, and simmer 20 to 30 minutes.

8 Puree cooked split peas in food processor or blender until smooth.

9 Remove bay leaves from soup and stir in split pea puree.

10 Bring to simmer and serve immediately.

★

MEXICAN CORN CHOWDER
YIELD: 8 SERVINGS

6 ears fresh corn
1 large purple onion

3 fresh green chile peppers (or small
can)

4 cloves garlic
1 bunch fresh cilantro
¼ cup unsalted margarine or butter
3 heaping tablespoons unbleached
    white flour
2 cups chicken stock

2 quarts milk
1 tablespoon cumin
2 teaspoons white pepper
salt to taste
pinch of crushed red pepper

1 Cut corn from cobs. Chop purple onion and green chiles. Mash and mince garlic. Finely chop cilantro and set aside.
2 Sauté onion, chile peppers, and garlic in margarine or butter over medium heat 5 to 7 minutes.
3 Add corn and cook 20 minutes over low flame, stirring frequently.
4 Add flour and stir an additional 5 to 10 minutes.
5 In another pot, bring chicken stock and milk to low simmer. Turn off heat under corn mixture.
6 Pour stock and milk into corn mixture in a steady stream, whipping constantly.
7 Return to low simmer and add chopped cilantro, cumin, white pepper, salt to taste, and crushed red pepper. Simmer 1 hour.
8 Serve with fresh cilantro leaf garnish.

★

HOT AND SOUR SOUP

YIELD: 6 SERVINGS

8–10 lily buds
2 tablespoons tree fungus or tree
    ears
9 cups strained unsalted chicken
    stock
2 whole chicken breasts
6 fresh water chestnuts, peeled and
    sliced, or ½ can
6 ounces bamboo shoots, cut into
    julienne strips
2 tablespoons grated and minced
    fresh ginger
3 cloves garlic, mashed and minced
2 green onions, chopped

½ teaspoon crushed red pepper
½ teaspoon Szechuan peppercorns,
    ground and strained
2 tablespoons sesame oil
3 tablespoons rice vinegar
1 teaspoon raw turbinado sugar
1 teaspoon tamari soy sauce
8 ounces tofu, cut into small cubes
3 egg whites
4 tablespoons arrowroot or
    cornstarch
¼ cup dry sherry
scallion greens, finely chopped, for
    garnish

1 Soak lily buds and tree fungus or ears in a cup of water for 30 minutes to 1 hour.
2 Bring chicken stock to simmer.
3 Skin, bone, and remove fat from chicken breasts. Slice chicken into thin strips and add to simmering stock.

4 Bring back to simmer and add water chestnuts, bamboo shoots, ginger, garlic, green onions, red pepper, Szechuan pepper, sesame oil, rice vinegar, sugar, and tamari soy sauce.

5 Bring back to simmer and add drained lily buds and tree fungus or ears, and simmer covered for 45 minutes.

6 Cut tofu into small cubes and add to stock. Simmer 15 minutes more.

7 Whip egg whites thoroughly and set aside.

8 In another container, thoroughly blend arrowroot or cornstarch and sherry. Slowly pour into simmering soup, then stir with a whisk 5 to 7 minutes.

9 Pour egg white mixture into soup with a circular motion. Turn off heat, cover, and let stand 5 to 10 minutes.

10 Serve in warmed soup bowls garnished with a pinch of freshly chopped scallion greens.

★

SOPA DE AJO

YIELD: 6 SERVINGS

3 canned green chile peppers
   (optional)
10 cloves garlic
1 teaspoon tamari soy sauce
¼ cup water
8 cups chicken broth

1 bunch cilantro
⅓ cup chopped scallion greens
3 egg whites
3 tablespoons cornstarch or
   arrowroot
¼ cup sherry

1 Remove seeds from canned green chiles and mash and mince 7 of the 10 cloves of garlic.

2 Combine green chiles, garlic, tamari soy sauce, and water in blender.

3 Mix with chicken broth in a soup pan and bring to simmer.

4 Slice remaining 3 garlic cloves. Separate cilantro leaves from stems and chop. Chop scallion greens. Add to simmering broth and simmer uncovered 30 minutes.

5 Slightly whip egg whites and set aside.

6 Mix cornstarch or arrowroot with sherry. Add to broth slowly, then stir constantly with whisk for 5 to 10 minutes, until it reaches desired consistency.

7 Pour egg whites into broth with a circular motion.

8 Turn off heat, cover, and let stand 5 minutes.

9 Serve garnished with sprigs of fresh cilantro.

★

COUNTRY-STYLE VEGETABLE SOUP

YIELD: 10–12 SERVINGS

2 cups chopped green beans
2 cups chopped celery
2 cups chopped carrots
2 onions
4 turnips
4 ears corn
3 tablespoons unsalted margarine
  or butter
3 medium potatoes

10 cups chicken or vegetable stock
¾ cup barley
1 14½-ounce can stewed tomatoes
pinch of sage
1 tablespoon thyme
½ teaspoon oregano
½ teaspoon celery seed
3 bay leaves
1 tablespoon ground red pepper

1 Coarsely chop green beans, celery, carrots, onions, and turnips. Slice fresh corn from the cob.
2 Heat margarine or butter in large soup pan and sauté vegetables, stirring often, over low heat.
3 Coarsely chop scrubbed, unpeeled potatoes and add to simmering vegetables. Cook 10 minutes.

4 Add stock, barley, and stewed tomatoes, stir, and bring to simmer.
5 Add sage, thyme, oregano, celery seed, bay leaves, and red pepper, and cook until vegetables are tender but not falling apart.

★

LEEK SOUP

YIELD: 6–8 SERVINGS

10–12 medium-sized leeks
4 tablespoons unsalted margarine
  or butter
1 tablespoon raw turbinado sugar
10 cups chicken or vegetable stock
2 tablespoons unbleached white
  flour

1 cup white wine
2 tablespoons Madeira wine
1 tablespoon Worcestershire sauce
¼ teaspoon cayenne pepper
dash of nutmeg
grated Parmesan cheese

1 Chop and wash leeks (see *Leeks*).
2 Melt margarine or butter in a large soup pan and add leeks. Simmer over low heat about 10 minutes.
3 Add sugar and simmer 20 minutes more, stirring very often.

4 While leeks are simmering, heat stock to low boil.
5 When leeks have cooked required time, add flour and stir constantly another 10 minutes.

6 Add hot stock to leek mixture and stir several minutes.

7 Add wines, Worcestershire sauce, cayenne pepper, and nutmeg and simmer covered for at least 1 hour. Slow, even cooking is the key to this soup.

8 Serve in warmed soup bowls sprinkled with Parmesan cheese. Can be served au gratin by topping soup with croutons and cheese and popping the bowls under the broiler to brown the cheese. Use ovenproof bowls!

★

PEPPER AND TOMATO SOUP
YIELD: 6 SERVINGS

1 pound poblano or mild green chile peppers
2 pounds red and/or green bell peppers
1 purple onion
6 cloves garlic
2 tablespoons olive oil
2 bay leaves

1 teaspoon chervil
1 teaspoon basil
1 teaspoon summer savory
4 cups unsalted tomato juice
4 cups chicken or vegetable stock
2 cups cooked brown rice (see Basic Grains, page 121)
fresh basil for garnish

1 Peel chiles (see Chile Peppers). Coarsely chop chiles, bell peppers, and onion into bite-size pieces.

2 Mash and mince garlic.

3 Heat olive oil to medium in large Dutch oven or soup pan and sauté peppers, onion, garlic, bay leaves, chervil, basil, and summer savory about 10 minutes.

4 After vegetables are cooked, combine tomato juice and stock in a separate pan, heat to simmer, and add to sautéed vegetables.

5 Simmer covered 45 minutes and remove from heat. Uncover and allow to cool somewhat.

6 In a blender or food processor, puree about half the soup mixture and return it to pan.

7 Stir in cooked brown rice and heat mixture to simmer. Thin with a bit of water if soup is too thick.

8 Serve in warmed bowls with a sprig of fresh basil on top.

★

OKRA GUMBO
YIELD: 6 SERVINGS

4 cups sliced okra
2 green peppers

1 purple onion
2 shallots

4 cloves garlic
6 stalks celery, including leaves
3 tablespoons unsalted margarine
   or butter
2 large tomatoes
pinch of fructose
1 teaspoon paprika
1 teaspoon Tabasco sauce

1 teaspoon thyme
1 teaspoon basil
1 bay leaf
freshly ground black pepper to taste
¼ teaspoon ground cloves
¼ teaspoon ground allspice
5 cups vegetable or chicken stock
3 teaspoons filé powder

1 Remove stems from okra, chop into
   ¼-inch pieces, and set aside.
2 Chop green peppers and onion;
   mince shallots, garlic, and celery.
   Combine with okra.
3 Melt margarine or butter in a cast-
   iron Dutch oven.
4 Add chopped and minced vegetables and cook about 7 minutes
   over medium heat.
5 While above vegetables are cooking, peel, seed, juice, and chop
   tomatoes. Add to cooking vegetables and cook 5 more minutes.

6 Add fructose, paprika, Tabasco
   sauce, thyme, basil, bay leaf, black
   pepper, cloves, and allspice and stir
   for about 1 minute.
7 Add stock and slightly increase
   heat. Cover and cook 45 minutes.
   Stir 2 or 3 times during cooking
   process.
8 Ladle into warmed bowls and sprinkle ½ teaspoon filé powder on top
   of each serving.

★

G A Z P A C H O

Y I E L D : 6 S E R V I N G S

4 bell peppers
4 cucumbers
2 stalks celery
4 whole green onions
3 cloves garlic
2 tablespoons fresh chopped parsley
6 large tomatoes
3 cups spicy tomato juice
juice of ½ lemon

juice of ½ lime
¼ cup champagne vinegar
½ teaspoon oregano
1 teaspoon coarsely ground black
   pepper
2 tablespoons olive oil
1 teaspoon (or more) Tabasco sauce
1 tablespoon paprika

1 Chop each vegetable ingredient by
   hand or in a food processor. Combine with other ingredients and
   chill 8 hours.

2 Serve in a chilled bowl.

★

EGG-LEMON SOUP WITH BARLEY

YIELD: 6 SERVINGS

8 cups chicken or vegetable stock
1 cup barley
1 cube unsalted vegetable bouillon
1 whole egg
2 egg whites

½ cup lemon juice
1 teaspoon white pepper
1 teaspoon Tabasco sauce
¼ teaspoon nutmeg
1 tablespoon minced parsley

1 Heat stock to simmering and add barley and crumbled bouillon cube. Simmer covered 40 minutes.

2 Place egg and egg whites in a blender and blend at high speed 2 minutes.

3 Add lemon juice and continue blending at high speed 1 minute.

4 With blender still running, slowly pour in 2 cups of hot barley mixture.

5 Remove soup pan from heat and pour in contents of blender while beating vigorously.

6 Serve immediately in warmed soup bowls garnished with ½ teaspoon minced parsley to each bowl.

7 To reheat this soup, carefully bring to a simmer over low heat. It can also be served cold.

FRUIT SOUPS

★

BLUEBERRY SOUP
YIELD: 6 SERVINGS

8 pints fresh blueberries (save a
   handful for garnish)
1 cup rosé wine
1 tablespoon dark rum

½ cup low-fat yogurt
2 tablespoons honey
2 cups ice water
½ teaspoon vanilla

1 Clean blueberries and remove
   stems.
2 Put wine, rum, and yogurt in
   blender or food processor and
   blend.
3 Add blueberries and puree. Put
   mixture in a bowl.
4 Blend in honey and then ice water
   and vanilla.

5 Put entire mixture through a
   strainer or food mill, and then
   strain through a fine sieve.
6 Chill at least 1 hour.
7 Serve in chilled bowls garnished
   with a dollop of yogurt and 2 or 3
   whole blueberries.

★

COLD CANTALOUPE SOUP
YIELD: 4 SERVINGS

1 medium cantaloupe, very ripe
¾ cup cold rosé wine
1 teaspoon vanilla extract

2 tablespoons fructose
½ cup yogurt
cinnamon for garnish

1 Halve, seed, quarter, and peel cantaloupe. Place in blender with cold
   rosé wine.
2 Add vanilla extract and fructose,
   and blend several minutes until
   very well pureed.

3 Add yogurt and blend thoroughly.
4 Chill 2 to 3 hours. Serve cold in a
   chilled bowl, with a very light
   sprinkling of cinnamon.

★

COLD CREAMY PEACH SOUP

YIELD: 4 SERVINGS

8 ripe peaches
¼ cup rosé wine
¼ cup cold water

½ cup yogurt
1 tablespoon fructose
1 tablespoon Amaretto liqueur

1 Peel, pit, and slice peaches.
2 Place in a blender with rosé wine and cold water. Blend at high speed until pureed.

3 Thoroughly blend in yogurt, fructose, and Amaretto.
4 Chill overnight.

★

COLD PUREE OF STRAWBERRY SOUP

YIELD: 6 SERVINGS

6 pints strawberries
1 cup low-fat yogurt
1 cup white grape juice
juice of 1 orange

½ teaspoon vanilla extract
2 teaspoons orange liqueur
4 tablespoons fructose
1 cup cold water

1 Wash, hull, and slice strawberries.
2 Combine strawberry slices with all other ingredients in a large bowl.
3 Puree mixture in 2 or 3 batches in a food processor or blender.
4 Strain pureed soup twice through a large sieve.

5 Chill at least 4 hours.
6 When ready to serve, whip soup thoroughly with a whisk to blend.
7 Serve in chilled bowls, preferably clear glass to highlight the color of the soup.

★

WARM CONSOMMÉ OF RASPBERRY

YIELD: 6 SERVINGS

8 pints fresh raspberries
8 cups light chicken stock
6 tablespoons low-fat yogurt

1 Puree raspberries with a little of the stock.
2 Place pureed raspberries in a large soup pan with the rest of the stock.

Simmer covered for 1 hour and strain.
3 Serve hot with a dollop of yogurt in each bowl.

4

SALADS, DRESSINGS, AND CONDIMENTS

SALADS

★

LOW-SODIUM CAESAR SALAD

Traditionally prepared tableside in restaurants.

YIELD: 6 SERVINGS

3 cloves garlic, peeled
1 teaspoon freshly ground black
* pepper*
½ teaspoon capers
1 teaspoon Dijon mustard
1 teaspoon Worcestershire sauce
1 whole egg

2 egg whites
1 cup virgin olive oil
4 tablespoons finely grated
* Parmesan cheese*
salad greens for 6 servings
Salad Croutons With Herbs (page
* 185)*

1 In a food processor or blender, or
in a ceramic or wooden bowl with
a wooden spoon, puree garlic and
black pepper.
2 Add capers and puree.
3 Add Dijon mustard and Worcestershire sauce and puree.
4 Add egg and egg whites and puree.

5 Slowly dribble in a few drops of
olive oil, increasing to a steady
stream and pureeing constantly until entire cup of oil is used.
6 Add Parmesan cheese and puree.
7 Toss with salad greens and garnish
with croutons. Serve immediately,
before salad wilts.

GUACAMOLE

YIELD: 6 SERVINGS

6 ripe avocados
juice of 2 lemons
1 tablespoon mayonnaise
1 tablespoon yogurt
1 tablespoon finely chopped green
* onion*

2 cloves garlic
6–8 dashes of Tabasco sauce
½ teaspoon cumin
salt and pepper

1 Select avocados that feel slightly
soft but not mushy. Peel and remove seeds. Save seeds to be used
later.

2 Place avocados in a mixing bowl
and sprinkle with juice of 1½
lemons. Mash with fork or electric
mixer until smooth.

3 Add mayonnaise and yogurt. Mix well.

4 Mince green onion and garlic and add to guacamole with Tabasco sauce, cumin, salt, and pepper. Stir until all ingredients are thoroughly blended.

5 Sprinkle with juice of ½ lemon and place avocado seeds on top of guacamole to prevent it from turning brown. Cover and refrigerate until ready to serve.

★

ROOT SALAD

The beets turn the dish pink.

YIELD: 4 SERVINGS

2 beets
½ cup peeled, cubed jicama
2 carrots

2 green onions
¾ cup Garlic Vinaigrette (page 93)

1 Boil beets until tender, then peel, slice, and chill.

2 Peel and cube jicama.

3 Cut carrots into ¼-inch slices on extreme bias.

4 Slice green onions.

5 Toss ingredients together and marinate in garlic vinaigrette in refrigerator until well chilled—1 to 2 hours.

★

TOMATO · ONION SALAD

YIELD: 6 SERVINGS

2 purple onions
4 tomatoes
1½ cups Garlic Vinaigrette
  (page 93)

fresh parsley for garnish

1 Cut purple onions into ¼-inch slices and separate into rings.

2 Cut tomatoes into ¼-inch slices.

3 Arrange both in bowl.

4 Marinate 2 hours in garlic vinaigrette.

5 Serve garnished with fresh parsley.

★

CARROT AND RAISIN SALAD

YIELD: 6 SERVINGS

6 medium carrots
1 cup raisins
2 tablespoons bran
¼ cup chopped almonds
1 tablespoon mayonnaise

1 tablespoon low-fat yogurt
¼ teaspoon almond extract
¼ cup pineapple juice or orange juice

1 Peel and grate carrots.
2 Combine all ingredients and mix well with a wooden spoon.

3 Cover and chill 1 to 2 hours before serving.

★

CURRIED BROWN RICE SALAD

YIELD: 6–8 SERVINGS

4 cups cooked brown rice (see Basic Grains, page 121)
2 cups fresh shelled English peas (1½ pounds unshelled)
2 cups cubed carrots (2 large)
4 cups seasoned stock
1 medium to large red bell pepper
2 stalks celery
1 green onion
3 tablespoons curry powder

½ teaspoon cayenne pepper
6 tablespoons mayonnaise
6 tablespoons low-fat yogurt
2 tablespoons white wine or champagne vinegar
½ teaspoon tamari soy sauce
8 ounces Havarti cheese
sprouts, watercress, or parsley for garnish

1 Cook rice.
2 Shell English peas and cut carrots into small cubes.
3 Bring stock to simmer and add peas and carrots. Cook 12 minutes. Drain and refresh in ice water.
4 Chop red bell pepper into small cubes and finely chop celery and green onion.
5 Mix rice, peas, carrots, bell pepper, celery, onion, curry powder, cayenne pepper, mayonnaise, yogurt, vinegar, and tamari soy sauce.
6 Cut cheese into small cubes and toss with salad.
7 Cover and place in refrigerator for 2 hours.
8 Serve garnished with sprouts, watercress, or parsley.

★

GARBANZO BEAN SALAD

Louise Koellhoffer

YIELD: 6 SERVINGS

1 pound garbanzo beans, cooked
   (see Basic Beans, page 121)
½ cup chopped parsley
¾ cup finely chopped purple onion
1 clove garlic
¼ cup lemon juice

2 tablespoons extra virgin olive oil
1 teaspoon sesame oil
2 teaspoons Tabasco sauce
1 teaspoon coarsely ground black
   pepper

1 Cook garbanzo beans and drain.
2 Chop parsley and onion. Mince garlic and toss all 3 ingredients with garbanzo beans in a mixing bowl.
3 Combine lemon juice, olive oil, sesame oil, Tabasco sauce, and pepper.

4 Pour dressing onto beans. Stir well to mix.
5 Cover and chill at least 4 hours.
6 Serve on a bed of spinach or other dark greens.

★

PEAR, WALNUT, AND WATERCRESS SALAD

YIELD: 6 SERVINGS

2–3 fresh pears in season
6 cups cleaned fresh watercress
   (about 5 or 6 commercial
   bunches)

¾ cup chopped walnuts
6 sliced radishes for garnish
cruets of pear vinegar and walnut
   oil for dressing

1 Peel and slice pears and treat with citrus juice (see *Fruit*).
2 Wash and dry watercress and arrange on salad plates.
3 Lay pear slices alongside watercress and sprinkle solid with walnuts.

4 Garnish with radish slices and serve with cruets of walnut oil and pear vinegar, as well as a pepper grinder.

★

AVOCADO, CITRUS, AND JERUSALEM ARTICHOKE SALAD

YIELD: 6 SERVINGS

2 ripe avocados
2 Texas Ruby Red grapefruits
2 large oranges
3 or 4 Jerusalem artichoke tubers

2 small heads Boston lettuce
Poppy Seed Dressing (page 95) or
*   Honey Mustard Salad Dressing*
*   (page 95)*

1 Peel avocados, cut into wedges, and dip into citrus juice to prevent discoloration.
2 Peel grapefruit and oranges and remove membranes from fruit segments (see *Fruit*).
3 Peel Jerusalem artichokes, slice, and cut into small julienne pieces.
4 Wash and dry Boston lettuce and finely shred.

5 On a serving platter or individual plates, mound chiffonade (shreds) of lettuce and arrange avocado, grapefruit, and orange slices around it attractively. Decorate with julienne of Jerusalem artichoke and serve with dressing.

★

TURKEY CABBAGE SLAW

YIELD: 6–8 SERVINGS

2 cups shredded green cabbage
6 green onions
2 cups grated carrots
juice of 1½ lemons
ice water
1 egg
1 teaspoon dry mustard
2 tablespoons fructose

2 teaspoons curry powder
1 tablespoon coarsely ground black
*   pepper*
1 clove garlic, minced
1 cup light oil
1 tablespoon whole fennel seed
¾ pound shredded smoked turkey
radishes for garnish

1 Shred cabbage; slice green onions lengthwise into small julienne strips; grate carrots. Combine in a large bowl.
2 Add juice of 1 lemon and enough ice water to cover. Refrigerate 1 or 2 hours.
3 Combine egg, juice of remaining ½

lemon, dry mustard, and fructose in a blender or food processor. Blend at high speed for a few seconds.
4 Add curry powder, black pepper, and minced garlic and blend again at high speed for a few seconds.
5 With the machine running, pour in oil in a slow stream.

6 Drain ice water from vegetables and toss with dressing and whole fennel seed.

7 Arrange shredded turkey on a serving platter and mound slaw in the middle. Garnish with radish slices.

★

WESTLAKE CHICKEN SALAD
YIELD: 8 SERVINGS

*8 whole chicken breasts
   (about 4 pounds)*
3 celery stalks
3 green onions
3 dill pickles
2 cloves garlic

*1 teaspoon coarsely ground black
   pepper*
1 tablespoon raspberry vinegar
1 teaspoon Tabasco sauce
1¼ cup mayonnaise

1 Split, skin, and bone chicken breasts and cook in a pan of already simmering water for 10 minutes. Make sure there is enough water to cover chicken. (Do not place chicken in cold water and bring to heat because this will leach out nutrients and flavor.)

2 While chicken is cooking, string celery and chop finely. Also chop green onions and dill pickles. Mash and mince garlic.

3 Combine celery, green onions, pickles, and garlic with black pepper, raspberry vinegar, and Tabasco sauce. Mix well and set aside.

4 Remove cooked chicken from pan and drain, reserving cooking liquid for stock.

5 When chicken is cool enough to handle, cut into small cubes with scissors or kitchen shears.

6 Combine cubed chicken with dressing. Blend well, cover, and refrigerate.

★

GAME BIRD SALAD
YIELD: 6–8 SERVINGS

*2 whole duck breasts or 12 quail
   breasts*
2 teaspoons white pepper
*2 medium yellow onions (2 cups
   coarsely chopped)*
6 cloves garlic
6 strips bacon

*½ cup Brown Poultry Stock
   (page 40)*
*2 large heads Boston or butter
   lettuce*
2 cups shredded spinach
*½ cup fresh shredded turnip or
   mustard greens*

*1 generous handful fresh basil
leaves*
½ cup dry red wine

1 Preheat oven to 375°.
2 Wipe breasts with damp cloth and rub inside and out with white pepper.
3 Coarsely chop onions and garlic and spread on the bottom of a roasting pan.
4 Place breasts skin side up on bed of onion and garlic. Cover each breast with 3 strips of bacon, add stock to roasting pan, and roast uncovered approximately 25 to 30 minutes at 375°.
5 While breasts are roasting, shred lettuce, spinach, turnip or mustard greens, and basil leaves; toss together. Arrange greens on individual plates and set aside in a cool place.

½ cup extra virgin olive oil
½ cup raspberry vinegar
freshly ground black pepper

6 Remove roasted breasts from pan and set aside in a warm place.
7 Add dry red wine to roasting pan. Deglaze pan and strain contents into a saucepan. Over medium heat, reduce liquid to 1 cup.
8 While sauce is reducing, bone breasts and slice meat into small pieces. Arrange on plates with greens.
9 Blend olive oil and raspberry vinegar with hot reduction and pour warm dressing across the top of the breast slices. The dressing should slightly wilt the greens.
10 Serve immediately, offering each guest freshly ground black pepper.

★

DILLED SHRIMP SALAD

YIELD: 6 – 8 SERVINGS AS ENTRÉE,
12 AS SALAD

3 pounds shrimp
juice of 2 lemons
juice of 1 lime
2 stalks celery
3 green onions

1 Peel, devein, and boil shrimp (see *Shrimp*).
2 Chop shrimp as desired (approximately ¼-inch pieces).
3 Place in a large bowl and add lemon and lime juice.
4 Finely chop celery, green onions, and pickle and add to shrimp. If

1 medium dill pickle
*1 heaping tablespoon dill weed
(preferably fresh)*
1 cup mayonnaise
white pepper

using fresh dill weed, chop finely before adding.
5 Stir in mayonnaise and season with white pepper to taste.
6 Stir well, cover, and allow to marinate in the refrigerator 2 hours. Set out 15 minutes before serving.

★

RAW CRANBERRY SALAD

YIELD: 6 – 8 SERVINGS

1 pound cranberries
1 cup raspberry or other fruit juice
2 packages unflavored gelatin
¾ cup fructose
juice and grated peel of 1 lemon

juice and grated peel of 1 orange
1 cup chopped celery
1 cup chopped unpeeled apples
1 cup chopped pecans
orange wedges for garnish

1 Rinse and pick over cranberries.

2 Heat fruit juice to simmering. Pour into mixing bowl and stir in gelatin and fructose.

3 Chill in refrigerator about 15 minutes, but do not allow to congeal.

4 Grate lemon and orange peel, juice fruit, and set aside.

5 Chop celery and unpeeled apples. Combine with peel and juice of lemon and orange.

6 Combine celery-apple mixture with cranberries and chopped pecans and fold into the syrupy gelatin mixture.

7 Pour into mold or serving dish and chill at least 2 hours.

8 Serve garnished with fresh orange wedges.

★

QUICK BANANA-NUT SALAD

Betty Wertz

YIELD: 1 SERVING

1 tablespoon chunky peanut butter
1 tablespoon honey
¼ cup mayonnaise

1 banana
lemon juice
candied fruit

1 Mix peanut butter and honey. Stir in mayonnaise.

2 Split banana in half lengthwise and dip in lemon juice.

3 Arrange banana on lettuce leaf and spread peanut butter mixture down the center of each half. Decorate with candied fruit.

DAIRY DRESSINGS

★

BUTTERMILK DRESSING

YIELD: ABOUT 2 CUPS

1 whole egg
1 egg yolk
1 tablespoon white vinegar
2 teaspoons Dijon mustard
1 teaspoon dried dill weed
1 small garlic clove, crushed
½ teaspoon thyme

½ teaspoon marjoram
½ teaspoon basil
½ teaspoon celery seed
½ cup vegetable oil
1 cup buttermilk
white pepper to taste

1 Combine egg and egg yolk in food processor.
2 Add white vinegar and Dijon mustard and blend thoroughly.
3 Add dill weed, garlic, thyme, marjoram, basil, and celery seed, and blend into dressing.
4 With machine running, slowly pour in vegetable oil.
5 Mix in buttermilk and season with white pepper to taste.

★

MOCK SOUR CREAM

My version of a recipe by Carol Hoke and Jo Ann Dabney. Serve as a condiment or use in recipes that call for sour cream.

YIELD: ABOUT 2 CUPS

4 tablespoons low-fat milk
1 tablespoon lime juice
1 tablespoon lemon juice

2 cups low-fat cottage cheese
¼ teaspoon white pepper
¼ teaspoon fructose

Blend all ingredients together in a blender or food processor until velvety smooth.

★

ROQUEFORT DRESSING

YIELD: 4 CUPS

2 eggs
¼ teaspoon white pepper
¼ teaspoon dry mustard
3 tablespoons red wine vinegar

½ teaspoon raw turbinado sugar
½ pound Roquefort cheese
1¼ cup oil (a good-tasting light oil)

1 Place all ingredients except cheese and oil into a blender or food processor and blend at high speed 2 minutes.
2 Crumble in Roquefort cheese.

3 With the machine running, slowly dribble in oil. Do not overblend. The dressing should not be smooth or too thick.
4 Add extra pepper and sugar to taste.

★

BUTTERMILK TOFU DRESSING

YIELD: 2½ CUPS

1 whole egg
1 egg white
1 teaspoon red wine vinegar
1 cup buttermilk
½ cup yogurt
1 heaping teaspoon prepared
   horseradish

1 teaspoon thyme
1 teaspoon black pepper
4 ounces tofu
½ cup light oil

1 In a food processor, blend egg, egg white, and wine vinegar for 1 minute.
2 Add buttermilk, yogurt, horse-radish, thyme, black pepper, and tofu, and blend another minute.
3 Slowly add oil while blending.

★

CREAMY SESAME DRESSING

YIELD: ABOUT 1½ CUPS

1 cup yogurt
½ cup tahini (sesame butter)
1 teaspoon tamari soy sauce
juice of ½ lemon

1 tablespoon toasted sesame seeds
Tabasco sauce to taste
1 teaspoon sesame oil

Blend all ingredients in a blender or food processor or by hand.

MAYONNAISE-BASED DRESSINGS

★

MAYONNAISE

The key to success in making this cold sauce in a blender is using fresh eggs and adding oil in a slow, steady stream.

YIELD: 4½ CUPS

1 whole egg
1 egg yolk
1 teaspoon dry mustard
1 tablespoon fructose

1 teaspoon white pepper
4 teaspoons wine vinegar
4 cups (approximate) good-tasting light vegetable oil

1 Place all ingredients except oil into a blender and blend at high speed 2 minutes.
2 Slowly dribble in oil until desired consistency is reached (the machine will begin to slow up).
3 Add extra pepper or fructose to taste.

Restoring Broken Mayonnaise

1 Remove the broken sauce from the blender and drop in 1 egg yolk.
2 Whirl it around for 60 seconds and slowly dribble the broken mayonnaise into the blender. It should restore itself perfectly.

★

THOUSAND ISLAND DRESSING

YIELD: 4 CUPS

1½ cups chopped celery
½ cup sweet pickle relish
1 tablespoon Worcestershire sauce
1 cup chili sauce, tomato table sauce, or ketchup

1 teaspoon Tabasco sauce
2 cups mayonnaise

Finely chop celery and stir together with other ingredients. If using food processor, chop celery coarsely and process quickly with other ingredients.

★

RANCH-STYLE DRESSING

YIELD: 4 CUPS

2 cups mayonnaise
2 cups low-fat yogurt
1 tablespoon dill weed

1 tablespoon thyme
1 tablespoon garlic powder
dash of Tabasco sauce

1 Blend together in blender or food processor or by hand.

2 Store in sealed container in refrigerator.

★

CHIPOTLE MAYONNAISE

Ramone Parras

YIELD: 2½ CUPS

2 cups mayonnaise
½ cup Salsa Chipotle (page 55)

Fold salsa into mayonnaise and serve as a dip for boiled shrimp or other seafood or as a spread for sandwiches.

VINAIGRETTES AND CREAMY VINAIGRETTES

★

VINAIGRETTE DRESSING

YIELD: ABOUT 1 CUP

3 cloves fresh garlic
½ cup wine vinegar
4 tablespoons extra virgin olive oil
juice of 1 lemon

½ teaspoon paprika
1 tablespoon Dijon mustard
2 tablespoons cracked black pepper
2 teaspoons Worcestershire sauce

1 Mash and mince garlic.
2 Combine garlic and all other ingredients in blender or food processor or whip by hand.

★

SOY-SESAME VINAIGRETTE

This dressing is especially good on Bibb or Boston lettuce.

YIELD: ABOUT ½ CUP

¼ cup oil
2½ tablespoons tarragon vinegar
2½ tablespoons tamari soy sauce
¼ teaspoon (tightly packed) fresh
  tarragon

¼ teaspoon dry mustard
⅛ teaspoon oriental sesame oil
freshly grated pepper to taste

Combine all ingredients and blend thoroughly by hand or in a blender or food processor.

★

GARLIC VINAIGRETTE

YIELD: 1½ CUPS

4 cloves garlic
1 egg
¼ cup red wine vinegar

½ teaspoon white pepper
¼ cup olive oil
¾ cup safflower oil

1 Peel and mash garlic.
2 Place in blender or food processor with egg, red wine vinegar, and white pepper and blend until smooth.

3 With the machine running, dribble in oil until the mixture is the consistency of very thin mayonnaise.

GREEN ONION VINAIGRETTE

This dressing will keep for several weeks in the refrigerator.

YIELD: ABOUT 3 CUPS

2 eggs
1 teaspoon dry mustard
1 teaspoon white pepper
½ cup champagne vinegar

1 bunch green onions
1 cup extra virgin olive oil
1½ cups vegetable oil

1 Place eggs, mustard, and white pepper into a blender or food processor and blend at high speed 1 to 2 minutes.
2 Add vinegar and onions while machine is running.

3 Slowly dribble in olive oil, followed by vegetable oil, until dressing is of a creamy consistency.

CHUNKY TOMATO VINAIGRETTE

YIELD: 1½ – 2 CUPS

6 ripe tomatoes
2 tablespoons extra virgin olive oil
¼ cup honey vinegar

½ teaspoon black pepper
2 cloves garlic, minced

1 Remove peel, core, juice, and seeds from tomatoes (see *Tomatoes*).
2 Chop tomatoes very coarsely and place into a food processor.
3 Blend 10 seconds or so and add

other ingredients. Blend for a few more seconds. Do not overprocess. Dressing should be chunky.
4 Serve with a green salad or refrigerate.

★

MUSTARD VINAIGRETTE

YIELD: 1½ CUPS

1 egg
1 tablespoon champagne vinegar

1 teaspoon white pepper
¼ cup Dijon mustard
1 cup salad oil

1 In a blender or food processor, combine egg, champagne vinegar, and white pepper. Blend at high speed 1 to 2 minutes.
2 Add Dijon mustard and blend another minute.

3 Slowly dribble in salad oil and turn off machine when mixture thickens.
4 Serve at room temperature.

★

HONEY MUSTARD SALAD DRESSING

YIELD: 1½ CUPS

1 egg
1 tablespoon champagne vinegar
1 tablespoon honey

1 teaspoon white pepper
¼ cup Dijon mustard
1 cup salad oil

1 In a blender or food processor, blend egg, champagne vinegar, honey, and white pepper at high speed 1 to 2 minutes.
2 Add Dijon mustard and blend another minute.

3 Slowly dribble in salad oil and turn off machine when mixture thickens.
4 Serve at room temperature.

★

POPPY SEED DRESSING

Mary Faulk Koock

YIELD: 4 CUPS

1 cup raw honey
2 teaspoons dry mustard
2 cups unrefined oil (safflower is light and nice)
3 tablespoons poppy seed

2 teaspoons sea salt (optional)
¾ cup cider vinegar
3 tablespoons onion juice
1 tablespoon lemon juice
1 teaspoon grated lemon peel

Combine all ingredients in blender or food processor and blend 1 minute.

★

CREAMY COUSCOUS VINAIGRETTE

YIELD: 2 – 2½ CUPS

1 cup cooked couscous
1¼ cup low-fat yogurt
1 tablespoon extra virgin olive oil
½ cup white wine or champagne
  vinegar
½ teaspoon fructose
½ teaspoon dry mustard
1 teaspoon white pepper

Flavorings (choose one)
½ cup chopped fresh herb, such as
  dill, parsley, etc., or
½ cup chopped green onions, or
3 cloves garlic, minced, or
mustard, avocado, tomatoes, or
  other additions to taste

1 Prepare couscous according to package instructions.
2 Puree all ingredients except flavoring in a blender for 5 minutes.

3 Add choice of flavorings and puree 2 more minutes.
4 Serve garnished with a sprig of some fresh herb.

★

CREAMY DILL AND YOGURT VINAIGRETTE

YIELD: 1½ CUPS

1 egg
¼ teaspoon dry mustard
1 teaspoon white pepper
juice of ½ lemon

2 tablespoons apple cider vinegar
3 tablespoons extra virgin olive oil
½ cup fresh dill weed
¾ cup low-fat yogurt

1 In a blender or food processor, combine egg, mustard, white pepper, lemon juice, and cider vinegar. Blend at high speed 1 to 2 minutes.
2 With the machine running, add olive oil in a slow, steady stream.

3 Add dill weed and puree until well blended.
4 Place yogurt in mixing bowl and fold in dill mixture.

LOW-OIL DRESSINGS

★

AVOCADO DRESSING
YIELD: ABOUT 4 CUPS

3 cups low-fat yogurt
2 tablespoons red wine vinegar
¼ teaspoon dry mustard
¼ teaspoon cumin

½ teaspoon white pepper
1 teaspoon fructose
1 ripe avocado
2 cloves garlic, minced

Combine all ingredients in food processor or blender and serve as salad dressing or dip for fresh vegetables.

★

DILL COTTAGE CHEESE DRESSING
YIELD: 2–3 CUPS

1 pound cottage cheese
½ cup (tightly packed) fresh dill weed
½ cup low-fat yogurt
juice of 2 lemons
4 tablespoons champagne vinegar

2 tablespoons extra virgin olive oil
2 teaspoons finely ground black pepper
2 teaspoons Worcestershire sauce
1 teaspoon tamari soy sauce

Combine all ingredients in blender or food processor and puree until smooth.

★

COTTAGE CHEESE—GREEN ONION DRESSING
YIELD: 2¼ CUPS

½ cup champagne vinegar
6 green onions or scallions
½ cup yogurt

1 cup low-fat cottage cheese
1 teaspoon black pepper
1 teaspoon tarragon

Combine all ingredients in blender or food processor and puree until smooth.

CONDIMENTS

★

HERB-FLAVORED VINEGAR

Use herbs such as basil, parsley, cilantro, rosemary, thyme, and marjoram, or pungent vegetables such as garlic and shallots, for this recipe.

YIELD: 2 LITERS

double handful of fresh whole herbs
2 liters light-tasting, good-quality

white wine vinegar or champagne
vinegar

1 Run a 2-liter glass container with a tight-fitting lid through dishwashing cycle or wash by hand in hot soapy water. Rinse carefully.
2 Wash fresh herbs and shake to remove excess water.

3 Warm vinegar in nonaluminum pan just to simmering.
4 Place herbs in clean jar and pour in hot vinegar.
5 Allow to cool. Then seal and age for 1 to 2 months.

★

POP LOWERY'S DILL PICKLES

YIELD: 6 QUARTS

2 cups whole fresh dill weed
6–12 cloves garlic
6–12 fresh cayenne or Tabasco
* peppers*
6 pinches of alum

small to medium cucumbers to fill 6
* quart jars*
1 quart vinegar
2 quarts water
1 cup salt

1 In each sterilized jar, place ⅓ cup dill weed, 1 or 2 cloves garlic, 1 or 2 peppers, and 1 pinch of alum.
2 Tightly pack cucumbers in jars.
3 Mix vinegar, water, and salt in a stockpot and bring to a boil.

4 Pour boiling mixture over cucumbers into jars.
5 Seal and allow to age 3 months.

★

BREAD AND BUTTER PICKLES

Betty Andrews

YIELD: 4 QUARTS

4 quarts sliced cucumbers
5 medium to large onions
½ cup salt
2 quarts ice
2 cups sugar

5 cups vinegar
1½ teaspoons turmeric
1 teaspoon celery seed
2 tablespoons dry mustard

1 Combine sliced cucumbers, onions, salt, and ice. Set aside for 3 hours.
2 Drain and rinse well.
3 Place in a pot and stir in sugar, vinegar, turmeric, celery seed, and mustard. Heat to boiling point, but do not boil.
4 Place in sterilized jars and seal.

★

TEXAS·PICKLED PEACHES

This pickle was one of my very special favorites as a child. It was served whenever we had fried chicken and always on holidays. Small ripe Stonewall peaches from the Texas Hill Country are perfect for this recipe, although any good, local peach will be nice. Do choose peaches small enough to fit easily into the jars.

YIELD: 4 QUARTS

12–14 small ripe, unblemished
  peaches
36–42 whole cloves (3 per peach)
2 cups dark brown sugar (will give
  peaches a dark color)

3 cups apple cider vinegar
1 cup water
4 cinnamon sticks
1 tablespoon whole allspice

1 Parboil peaches 3 to 4 minutes and dip into cold water to remove skins quickly, but do not remove stones.
2 Stud each peach with 3 whole cloves. Set aside.
3 In a large stainless steel or enameled pan, combine brown sugar, vinegar, water, and cinnamon sticks. Cover and bring to a low boil.
4 Add peaches 3 or 4 at a time, and cook all together about 10 minutes.
5 Allow peaches to stand in liquid 4 to 6 hours.
6 Spoon peaches into hot, sterilized, wide-mouth jars.
7 Bring syrup to a boil. Place 1 stick of cinnamon into each jar and cover with hot syrup, leaving a little space at the top of each jar.
8 Place seals and lids on immediately. Allow to settle and cool.
9 Store peaches in refrigerator and allow to age at least a month.

5

VEGETABLES

★

BRAISED ARTICHOKES

Ann Clark, La Bonne Cuisine School

YIELD: 6 – 8 SERVINGS

6 artichokes
½ teaspoon salt
2 small yellow onions
2 carrots
3 cloves garlic
2 tablespoons extra virgin olive oil
2 tablespoons unsalted butter

1–2 large tomatoes
1–2 teaspoons thyme
2 tablespoons chopped parsley
⅛ teaspoon pepper
1 imported bay leaf
1–1½ cups chicken broth
1–1½ cups dry white wine

1 Trim, quarter, and remove choke from artichokes.
2 Bring a 6-quart pot of water to a boil. Add salt and artichokes, and blanch 7 to 10 minutes. Remove and drain.
3 Chop yellow onions and carrots. Mash garlic.
4 In a large, heavy casserole, sauté onions, carrots, and garlic in olive oil and butter until they take on color.
5 Seed and chop tomatoes. Add to sauté.
6 Add thyme, parsley, pepper, and bay leaf. Mix well.
7 Add broth and wine, then add artichokes. Cover and simmer 1 to 1¼ hours on top of stove or in a 325° oven.

★

CLASSIC ASPARAGUS

YIELD: 4 – 6 SERVINGS

1½ pounds fresh asparagus (about 30–36 spears)

Hollandaise Sauce (page 46)
fresh lemon wedges for garnish

1 Wash each asparagus stalk and snap off the bottom stems where they will break. Tie asparagus into a standing bundle with kitchen twine.
2 Use a tall and narrow pan if possible, at least as tall as the asparagus. Pour 2 to 3 inches of water in the pan. Place the bundle of asparagus in the middle of the pan. Bring to a boil and cover.
3 Continue boiling 8 to 10 minutes. Test for doneness. Asparagus should be tender, yet slightly crunchy. Do not overcook.
4 Serve with hollandaise sauce. Garnish with lemon wedges.

★
BRAISED ASPARAGUS TIPS WITH RASPBERRY VINEGAR

YIELD: 6 SERVINGS

4 cups asparagus tips (about 2 inches long)
3 tablespoons unsalted margarine or butter

2 tablespoons water or stock
¼ cup raspberry vinegar
1 teaspoon coarsely ground red pepper

1 Slice the top 2 inches off the asparagus spears and save stalks for a soup, soufflé, or other dish.
2 Melt margarine or butter in a large sauté pan.
3 Add asparagus tips and stir a bit. Cook over medium heat 3 minutes.

4 Add water, vinegar, and red pepper and continue cooking over medium heat, stirring now and then.
5 About the time the liquid cooks off, the asparagus should be ready. Serve immediately, simply garnished.

★
STRING BEANS WITH FLAVORED BUTTERS

One of the great American contributions to cooking. In season, fresh beans need little glorification.

YIELD: 4 SERVINGS

1 pound fresh string beans
3 cups water
juice of ½ lemon

bowl of ice water
½ cup flavored margarine or butter (pages 43–45)

1 Wash beans, snap off tips, and remove strings. Break into 2-inch pieces.
2 Bring water and lemon juice to a boil. Add beans and boil 8 to 10 minutes (or to taste).
3 Immerse hot beans in ice water to stop cooking process. Drain and set aside until ready to be heated with

flavored margarine or butter and served.
4 Melt margarine or butter in a large skillet or pan. When it starts to foam, add cooked string beans and cook 3 to 5 minutes, just enough to heat the beans.
5 Serve garnished with fresh herbs.

★

COUNTRY-STYLE BEETS

YIELD: 4–6 SERVINGS

1½ pounds fresh beets
unsalted margarine or butter and
  seasonings to taste

orange slices for garnish

1 Carefully wash beets and remove greens if still attached.
2 Place beets into a deep pan with water to cover, bring to a boil, and cover. Boil 50 minutes to 1 hour or until tender. Timing will depend on size.
3 When beets are tender, remove from heat and pour off water. Slice off leaf crown and little root. Skin should slide off rather easily.
4 Slice hot beets and serve quickly with margarine or butter and seasonings. Garnish with a thin orange round.

★

DILL-BRAISED CABBAGE WEDGES

YIELD: 8 SERVINGS

1 medium head green cabbage
3 tablespoons unsalted margarine
  or butter
3 cloves garlic
2 tablespoons chopped fresh dill
  weed

Tabasco sauce
black pepper
1 cup white wine
1 cup water
8 sprigs fresh dill weed for garnish

1 Wash cabbage and peel away any discolored leaves. Cut in half and core. Cut each half into 4 wedges.
2 Arrange cabbage wedges in a large, deep skillet.
3 Dot each wedge with bits of the margarine or butter.
4 Mince garlic and chop dill weed and sprinkle on top of cabbage wedges.
5 Top each wedge with a generous dash of Tabasco and a sprinkling of black pepper.
6 Add white wine and water.
7 Cover and braise over a medium flame about 15 minutes. Cabbage should be tender but not wilted or mushy.
8 Garnish each wedge with a sprig of dill weed and serve immediately with dill or other herb-flavored vinegar (page 98).

★

BRAISED SAVOY CABBAGE

YIELD: 6–8 SERVINGS

1 *head savoy cabbage*
2 *tablespoons unsalted margarine*
  or butter
2 *cups white wine*
2 *cups chicken or vegetable stock or*
  water
2 *tablespoons fruit vinegar*
  (raspberry, cherry, pear, etc.)

½ *teaspoon cayenne pepper*
½ *teaspoon white pepper*
pinch of thyme
pinch of tarragon
pinch of nutmeg
salt or tamari soy sauce (optional)

1 Shred or grate cabbage.
2 Melt margarine or butter in a large skillet and add cabbage. Stir constantly 2 to 3 minutes, then add all other ingredients except salt or tamari soy sauce.
3 Cook until most of the liquid has evaporated and cabbage is tender, but not wilted or soggy.
4 Season to taste with salt or tamari soy sauce.
5 Serve immediately with cruets of vinegar and hot pepper sauce.

★

HONEY-GLAZED CARROTS

This vegetable recipe could easily be a dessert.

YIELD: 6 SERVINGS

1 *pound fresh carrots*
4 *tablespoons unsalted margarine*
  or butter
1 *tablespoon bourbon*

2 *tablespoons locally produced*
  honey
½ *teaspoon cinnamon*
¼ *cup chopped pecans*

1 Select small tender carrots if possible, and scrub them carefully. Do not peel.
2 Slice carrots into ½-inch rounds or julienne strips.
3 Barely cover with water in a saucepan and bring to a boil. Cook about 15 minutes and remove pan from heat.
4 Drain, reserving liquid for stock.
5 In a large skillet or sauté pan, heat margarine or butter gently, allowing it to foam.
6 Add carrots and coat evenly with hot margarine or butter.
7 Stir in bourbon and cook for a couple of minutes.
8 Add honey and cinnamon. Cook carrots over low heat until done, stirring often to cover carrots with glaze.
9 Remove from heat and serve topped with chopped pecans.

★

CAULIFLOWER AND CHEESE

YIELD: 6 SERVINGS

1 head cauliflower
2 cups grated cheddar cheese

1 Trim and wash cauliflower and submerge upside down in a pan of boiling water.

2 Simmer 8 to 10 minutes. Meanwhile, preheat oven to 400°.

3 Remove cauliflower and drain thoroughly.

4 Place in buttered casserole dish and pack 2 cups grated cheddar cheese on top.

5 Place in oven and serve when cheese starts to bubble and brown.

★

CORN ON THE COB

YIELD: 8 SERVINGS

8 fresh ears of corn
unsalted margarine or butter
seasoning of choice

1 Remove husks and silk from corn.

2 Bring large pan of water to a boil.

3 Carefully drop ears of corn into water and boil about 10 minutes. Test for tenderness.

4 Remove from water and serve with margarine or butter and seasonings. (Try lemon juice instead of salt.)

★

MARINATED CUKES AND ONIONS

This is an old favorite of my mother's. It's best in the summertime with garden-fresh vegetables and herbs.

YIELD: 6 CUPS

1½ cups champagne vinegar or
* other light vinegar*
1 cup ice water
1 cup ice cubes
3 medium cucumbers
1 large purple onion

½ teaspoon whole cloves
½ teaspoon coarsely ground white
* pepper*
1 handful fresh dill weed
1 handful fresh parsley

1 In an 8-cup glass container with a lid, combine vinegar, ice water, and ice.
2 Peel cucumbers and onion and slice into ¼-inch rounds. Toss together in vinegar mixture.

3 Place cloves, pepper, and fresh herbs on top.
4 Cover and refrigerate 4 to 6 hours.

★

SAUTÉED FRESH CORN WITH TURMERIC

YIELD: 6 SERVINGS

12 medium ears of corn
2 tablespoons extra virgin olive oil
½ teaspoon cayenne pepper
¼ teaspoon nutmeg

1 teaspoon finely ground black pepper
1 teaspoon turmeric
½ cup dry white wine

1 Shuck corn and slice kernels from cobs.
2 Heat olive oil in a large skillet, add corn kernels, and sauté over medium heat.
3 Cook 5 minutes, then add cayenne pepper, nutmeg, pepper, and turmeric.

4 Cook 10 more minutes, stirring often.
5 Add wine and cook until liquid in pan is almost evaporated.
6 Serve on a warmed serving platter with a red garnish—radish flower, tomato rose, paprika, etc.

★

FRESH GREENS

Use mustard, turnip, collard, or other available greens for this recipe.

YIELD: 4–6 SERVINGS

1½ pounds (at least) fresh greens
2 cloves garlic
1 small onion
water or stock to cover
1 tablespoon unsalted margarine or butter

1 bay leaf
¼ teaspoon cayenne pepper
juice of 1 lemon
2 hard-boiled eggs, sliced, for garnish

1 Soak fresh greens in cool water 20 to 30 minutes to loosen sand. Then rinse under running water.
2 With a sharp knife, remove large stems from greens.

3 Chop garlic and onion and combine them in a large pot with greens, water or stock, margarine or butter, bay leaf, cayenne pepper, and lemon juice.

4 Bring to a low simmer and cover. Cook 20 to 30 minutes, depending on size of fresh greens.

5 When greens are tender, remove from heat and pan. Reserve the pot liquor for drinking or soups.

6 Serve garnished with hard-boiled egg slices, and offer cruets of herb-flavored vinegar (page 98).

★

SAUTÉED MUSHROOMS IN RED WINE

YIELD: 6 SERVINGS

1½ pounds fresh small mushrooms
4 chopped shallots
2 tablespoons extra virgin olive oil
1 teaspoon thyme
2 teaspoons coarsely ground black pepper

1 tablespoon Worcestershire sauce
½ teaspoon Dijon mustard
⅓ cup dry red wine

1 Wash and clean mushrooms but leave whole. Finely chop shallots.

2 Heat olive oil in a sauté pan, add chopped shallots, and stir 1 minute over high heat.

3 Reduce heat to low. Add mushrooms and cook for about 2 more minutes.

4 Add thyme, black pepper, Worcestershire sauce, and Dijon mustard and cook for 5 minutes.

5 Add red wine and increase heat. When cooking liquid has almost evaporated, mushrooms are ready to be served.

★

STEAMED OKRA WITH ONIONS AND RED BELL PEPPERS

Diane Roberts

YIELD: 4–6 SERVINGS

2 pounds small, tender fresh okra
1 small red bell pepper
1 small white onion

2 tablespoons unsalted margarine or butter
freshly ground black pepper to taste

1 Closely trim stems from okra pods, taking care to leave the whole pod intact. Arrange okra in steamer so that the thickest part is toward the bottom and center of the steamer.

2 Cut red bell pepper and white onion into julienne strips and scatter strips on top of okra.

3 Place the steamer in a pan containing about 1 inch of water and bring

water to a boil. Then reduce heat to medium and steam 4 to 5 minutes. The okra should turn bright green.

4 Remove vegetables from steamer and toss with margarine or butter.
5 Season with coarsely ground black pepper to taste.

★

FRESH KENNEDALE BLACK-EYED PEAS

I can still distinctly remember picking fresh peas at my grandfather's farm in North Texas. After picking the peas, we washed, shelled, and snapped them. Boiling them in a savory broth completed the summer ritual.

YIELD: 4–6 SERVINGS

1½ pounds fresh black-eyed peas
4 cups water or stock
1 medium white onion

3 cloves garlic
2 tablespoons safflower oil
salt and pepper if desired

1 Wash peas. Shell mature ones, snap smaller ones.
2 Combine with water or stock in a large pan and bring to a boil.
3 While peas are heating, coarsely chop onion and finely mince garlic.

Add to peas along with safflower oil.
4 When peas begin to boil, cover pan and boil 20 to 25 minutes. Test for doneness and season to taste.

★

ENGLISH PEAS

YIELD: 4–6 SERVINGS

2 pounds fresh English peas
4 cups water or stock
¼ cup (loosely packed) fresh parsley leaves

3 tablespoons unsalted margarine or butter
1 tablespoon coarsely ground green peppercorns

1 Shell peas while bringing water or stock to a boil.
2 Add peas and cook uncovered 7 to 10 minutes.
3 While peas are cooking, chop pars-

ley. Test peas for tenderness and drain, reserving liquid for stock.
4 Toss cooked peas with margarine or butter and green peppercorns, and serve topped with chopped parsley.

★

SNOW PEAS WITH FRESH GINGER

Also known as the sugar pea, this vegetable is a widely recognized element in oriental cookery. Snow peas are high in protein and other nutrients. Serve this dish hot as part of an oriental menu or experiment with combining dishes to suit your preference.

YIELD: 6 SERVINGS

1 pound fresh snow peas
2 tablespoons safflower oil
1 clove garlic
2 tablespoons grated and minced
  fresh ginger
1 tablespoon toasted sesame oil

½ teaspoon cayenne pepper
¼ cup dry white wine
1 tablespoon arrowroot
1 teaspoon tamari soy sauce
2 tablespoons water or stock

1 Wash peas. Break off the tips and remove tough strings that run along the sides.
2 Either steam peas or immerse them in boiling water for about 2 minutes.
3 Remove from heat, strain, and plunge into a bowl of ice water to stop cooking process.
4 Mince garlic. Peel, grate, and finely mince ginger.
5 Heat oil in a wok, then add garlic and ginger. Cook about 1 minute, stirring constantly.

6 Add cooled snow peas and stir for a minute.
7 Stir in sesame oil and cayenne pepper.
8 Combine white wine, arrowroot, tamari soy sauce, and water or stock and blend well.
9 When peas are hot, add arrowroot mixture and stir constantly about 3 more minutes, until snow peas are coated with light sauce.

HERBED STEAMED NEW POTATOES

Efficient and healthful steam cooking is further enhanced by aromatic herbs in the cooking water.

YIELD: 4 SERVINGS

1 pound small new potatoes
1 handful fresh herbs or *2*
  tablespoons dried herbs (parsley,
  dill weed, basil, sage, tarragon, or
  combination)

seasonings and unsalted margarine
  or butter to taste

1 Scrub potatoes and remove any blemishes.
2 Arrange potatoes in metal or bamboo steamer.
3 Place steamer over a small amount of water into which you have placed the herbs. Cover and steam 15 to 18 minutes.
4 Serve with choice of seasonings, margarine or butter, and sprigs of fresh herb as garnish.

★

BASIC BAKED POTATO

YIELD: 1 SERVING

1 Idaho russet baking potato
2 teaspoons olive oil
1/4 teaspoon leaf thyme

1/4 teaspoon white pepper
pinch of oregano

1 Wash and scrub potato. Pat dry and remove any blemishes.
2 Coat potato with olive oil and sprinkle with thyme, white pepper, and oregano.
3 Place potato on baking sheet to catch the oil.
4 Bake at 425° 1½ to 2 hours.

5 To prepare potato for serving, wrap in towel and roll between your hands, squeezing gently.
6 Remove towel and cut a lengthwise slit about halfway through the potato. Push ends of potato toward each other to open slit.

★

TWICE-BAKED POTATOES

YIELD: 8 SERVINGS

4 large baked potatoes
1/4 cup low-fat milk
1 tablespoon unsalted margarine or butter
2 cups grated cheddar cheese
1/2 cup Mock Sour Cream (page 89) or sour cream

1 teaspoon black pepper
1 teaspoon garlic powder
chopped greens from 8 green onions
1/4 cup pine nuts

1 Bake potatoes. Allow to cool enough to work with comfortably.
2 Slice potatoes in half and scoop out most of the flesh into a mixing bowl.
3 Add milk and margarine or butter.

Beat with an electric mixer until smooth.
4 Stir in 1½ cups of grated cheese, using a wooden spoon. Reserve remaining ½ cup of cheese for sprinkling on top of finished potatoes.

5 Stir in mock sour cream or sour cream, pepper, garlic powder, green onion tops, and pine nuts.
6 Refill baked potato shells with mixture, sprinkle with cheese, and bake at 400° for 20 minutes. Serve immediately.

★

MONTANA POTATO LOAF

Chloe Roosma

YIELD: 6 SERVINGS

3 large potatoes
3 large purple onions
3 cups grated Swiss cheese
4 egg whites

¼ cup finely chopped parsley
2 teaspoons coarsely ground black
    pepper
paprika

1 Preheat oven to 400°.
2 Grate raw potatoes, onions, and cheese. Combine in a mixing bowl.
3 Whip egg whites slightly and stir into cheese-onion-potato mixture.
4 Stir in parsley and black pepper.
5 Place in a 9-by-12-inch baking dish with glass cover (or cover with foil after next step).
6 Sprinkle with paprika and bake covered in a hot oven about 1 hour. Remove cover or foil during last 15 minutes to brown the top.

★

GOOD EAST TEXAS YAMS

From the original instructions for Georgia Stokley's family recipe: "This yam dish is really good, and can be made beautifully, but be sure you have some good East Texas yams."

YIELD: 8 SERVINGS

4 large yams
juice and peel of 1 lemon
2 cups fructose
2 cups orange juice

3 teaspoons cornstarch
3 tablespoons unsalted margarine
    or butter
orange slices for garnish

1 Try to select yams that are uniform in size. Peel and place in cold water to cover. Add lemon juice and chopped peel.
2 Cover pan and cook yams slowly until they are tender, yet firm.
3 While yams are cooking, combine fructose, orange juice, and cornstarch in top section of a double boiler and stir until glaze becomes very thick. Remove from heat and let stand.

4 Slice cooled yams into ¼-inch rounds. Spread in about 2 layers in a baking dish and dot with margarine or butter.

5 Spread glaze over yams and cover with thin orange slices. Heat in 350° oven and serve.

DIXIE SWEET POTATOES

Betty Wertz

YIELD: 6 SERVINGS

2 cups mashed sweet potatoes
2 eggs, beaten
½ cup honey

½ cup chopped pecans
¾ teaspoon salt
orange slices for garnish

1 Preheat oven to 350°.
2 Thoroughly mix all ingredients and bake in an 8-inch baking dish about 30 minutes.

3 Garnish with orange slices.

STEAMED ACORN SQUASH

This is a basic but very tasty way of preparing acorn squash, using just butter and pepper. But you may cut the steaming time in half and the squash will be ready to be filled with any number of delicious stuffing mixtures and baked.

YIELD: 2 SERVINGS

1 acorn squash
unsalted margarine or butter
white pepper

1 Wash squash, cut in half, and remove seeds.
2 Arrange squash halves cut side down in a steamer and steam about 40 minutes or until tender (20 min-

utes if squash is to be stuffed and baked).
3 Serve with white pepper and margarine or butter.

★
SPAGHETTI SQUASH

When properly cooked, the firm flesh of this squash becomes rather stringy and resembles spaghetti; hence the name. Use the cooked squash with any sauce for pasta or toss lightly with butter and pepper. Its delicate flavor blends easily with a number of dishes.

YIELD: 4–6 SERVINGS

1 3-pound spaghetti squash
seasoning to taste
2–3 cups pasta sauce (optional)

1 Wash squash and cut into quarters.
2 Place in steamer and steam about 20 minutes. Squash is done when it separates into stringy strands when tested with a fork.
3 Scrape cooked squash with a fork and place the strands into a warmed bowl.
4 Toss with seasonings and margarine or butter and serve topped with your choice of pasta sauces.

★
AUSTIN SQUASH CASSEROLE

YIELD: 8 SERVINGS

3 medium to large yellow squash
3 medium to large zucchini squash
2 medium onions
1 bell pepper
3 cloves garlic
½ cup bread crumbs
1 tablespoon thyme
1 teaspoon white pepper
1 egg yolk
3 egg whites
1 cup crème fraîche
½ cup grated Muenster cheese
¼ cup grated Parmesan cheese

1 Preheat oven to 400°.
2 Slice squash into ½-inch rounds. Cut onions into ½-inch slices and separate into rings. Slice bell pepper into ½-inch rings. Slice garlic thinly.
3 Combine bread crumbs, thyme, and white pepper and toss with vegetables.
4 Mix in a separate bowl with a whisk: egg yolk, egg whites, crème fraîche, and grated Muenster cheese.
5 Pour over vegetable mixture and toss thoroughly.
6 Pour into buttered casserole dish.
7 Sprinkle with grated Parmesan cheese.
8 Cover and bake at 400° for 1½ hours.
9 Remove cover and serve in same dish.

★

CALABACITAS

Juana Hargrove

A Mexican dish that is probably Indian in origin (except for the cheese).

Y I E L D : 4 – 6 S E R V I N G S

2 pounds zucchini or yellow squash
¼ cup chopped green onions
3 tablespoons extra virgin olive oil
¼ cup low-fat milk
2 cups corn (fresh or frozen)

canned or roasted and peeled fresh
   green chile peppers (see Chile
   Peppers*) to taste*
1 cup grated white cheddar cheese

1 Slice squash into bite-size pieces and chop onions.
2 In a cast-iron skillet, combine squash, onions, olive oil, and milk. Cover skillet and simmer a few minutes.
3 If frozen corn is used, add now. With fresh corn, slice from cob and add when squash becomes somewhat translucent.

4 Cover and simmer until corn is tender.
5 Add green chiles to taste. Cover and let simmer 1 minute more. Remove from heat.
6 Stir in grated cheese and cover skillet. Allow to sit a few minutes and serve when cheese is melted.

★

FORT WORTH SQUASH CASSEROLE

Marianne Lowery

Y I E L D : 6 S E R V I N G S

4–5 medium yellow or zucchini
   squash (about 1 pound)
½ cup chopped onion
½ cup chopped green bell pepper
½ cup chopped celery
¼ cup unsalted margarine or butter
1 cup sliced water chestnuts

2 eggs, slightly beaten
1 tablespoon mayonnaise
1 tablespoon fructose
dash of cayenne pepper
¼ cup grated cheddar cheese
¼ cup grated Parmesan cheese
¼ cup bread crumbs

1 Preheat oven to 350°.
2 Slice squash and boil or steam until slightly soft.
3 Remove from heat, drain, and mash

with a fork or potato masher. Set aside.
4 Chop onion, green bell pepper, and celery.

5 Melt margarine or butter in skillet and sauté onion, bell pepper, and celery 4 to 5 minutes. Add to squash mixture.

6 Then add sliced water chestnuts, slightly beaten eggs, mayonnaise, fructose, and cayenne pepper.

7 Stir well and pour into buttered 9-by-12-inch baking dish.

8 Top with grated cheeses and bread crumbs and bake at 350° for 30 minutes.

★

B A K E D   S T U F F E D   T O M A T O E S

These tomatoes must be served immediately because they do not keep well once baked.

Y I E L D : 6 S E R V I N G S

¼ cup unsalted margarine or butter
6 large tomatoes (ripe but not mushy)
1 cup grated Havarti cheese
½ cup ricotta cheese
1 cup toasted whole wheat bread crumbs
⅓ cup lightly toasted pine nuts
1 egg

2 cloves garlic
¼ teaspoon cayenne pepper
1 teaspoon thyme
2 teaspoons dill weed
1 teaspoon finely ground black pepper
2 tablespoons grated Parmesan cheese

1 Preheat oven to 350°.

2 Melt margarine or butter and remove from heat.

3 Slice off stem end of tomato. If necessary to make tomato sit level, cut off small slice from bottom. From stem end, hollow out about ⅔ of the pulp with tomato shark, grapefruit spoon, or paring knife. Do not break skin.

4 Baste hollowed-out tomatoes inside and out with melted margarine or butter.

5 Place tomatoes open end up in baking dish.

6 Grate Havarti cheese and combine with ricotta cheese, bread crumbs, pine nuts, and egg.

7 Mash and mince garlic and add to rest of filling along with cayenne pepper, thyme, dill weed, and black pepper.

8 Stir mixture until well blended and stuff into hollow tomatoes. Smooth off tops of tomatoes and sprinkle with Parmesan cheese.

9 Cover with foil and bake 20 to 25 minutes at 350°. Remove foil for the last 5 minutes to allow tops to brown nicely.

★

STIR-FRIED VEGETABLES IN A WOK

Stir-frying is an ancient oriental method of cooking small pieces of food in hot oil in a wok, a wide, shallow pan with handles that sits on a metal ring over the fire. In the Orient, it is used as deep fryer, skillet, saucepan, and even soup kettle.

YIELD: 4 SERVINGS

1 medium chopped onion
1 cup shredded cabbage
1 pound mushrooms or *3 cups of any vegetable*
¼ cup sesame oil

6 ounces cubed tofu (optional)
1 tablespoon tamari soy sauce
1 tablespoon minced fresh ginger
¼ cup water
2 tablespoons arrowroot

1 Chop vegetables and prepare other ingredients.
2 Heat sesame oil in the wok. The oil must be hot before you add anything.
3 Add all vegetables except tofu and stir over high heat.
4 If using tofu cubes, add after other

ingredients are almost done and stir gently another 2 minutes.
5 At the last minute, add tamari soy sauce, ginger, and water blended with arrowroot.
6 Cook a minute or so more, until the sauce turns thick.

6

GRAINS, LEGUMES, AND PASTAS

SIDE DISHES AND ENTRÉES

★

BASIC GRAINS

Grains are a truly universal staple, wheat and barley probably having been cultivated the longest. All of the grains listed are extremely nutritious and, properly served, a creative addition to a menu.

YIELD: 2−4 SERVINGS

Grain	Amount	Margarine, Butter, Or Oil	Stock	Salt (Optional)	Time
Barley	1 cup	1 tbsp.	2 cups	½ tsp.	1 hr.
Brown rice	1 cup	1 tbsp.	2 cups	½ tsp.	50−60 min.
Cracked wheat	1 cup	1 tbsp.	2 cups	½ tsp.	20 min.
Millet	1 cup	1 tbsp.	3 cups	½ tsp.	35 min.
Rye (groats)	1 cup	1 tbsp.	3 cups	½ tsp.	50−60 min.
Wheat berries	1 cup	1 tbsp.	2 cups	½ tsp.	3 hr.

Method 1: Combine all ingredients and bring to a boil. Cover and reduce heat. Simmer until done (see table for times).

Method 2: Bring stock to a low boil. Meanwhile, sauté grain in butter, margarine, or oil for 3 minutes, stirring constantly. Add boiling stock to grain, then add other ingredients. Bring mixture to a boil, cover, and cook over moderately low heat until done (see table for times).

★

BASIC BEANS

Beans are full of nourishment, inexpensive, and a must for most of our favorite cuisines. Use garbanzos, pintos, reds, whites, navies, black-eyed peas, or other common dried legumes for this recipe.

YIELD: 4 SERVINGS

1 cup dried beans
3 cups stock

1 medium onion
3 cloves garlic

1 tablespoon oil
1 bay leaf
1 teaspoon thyme

*½ teaspoon coarsely ground black
    pepper*

1 Pick over beans and rinse in a sieve
or colander.
2 Place beans in a pan with water to
cover, and allow to soak overnight.
3 Drain, rinse, and combine with
stock in a covered saucepan. Bring
to a boil.
4 Chop onion and mince garlic. Add
to boiling beans along with oil, bay
leaf, thyme, and black pepper.

5 Simmer covered about 2 hours.
6 Season to taste after cooking.

*Note: The following require different
cooking times.*
    aduki and mung beans: 1 hour,
        unsoaked
    lentils: 1 hour, unsoaked
    split peas: 45 minutes, unsoaked
    soybeans: 4 hours, soaked

★

SAFFRON BROWN RICE

YIELD: 6 SERVINGS

2 cups brown rice
4 cups unsalted chicken stock
few strands of saffron

*1 tablespoon unsalted margarine or
    butter*

1 Combine all ingredients in a covered saucepan.
2 Cook covered over medium heat
50 to 60 minutes and allow to
stand covered 20 minutes.

3 Uncover, fluff with fork, and serve
garnished with pimiento strips, paprika, or something else colorful.

★

BROWN RICE PILAF

YIELD: 6–8 SERVINGS

*2 tablespoons unsalted margarine
    or butter*
2 cups brown rice
6 cups chicken or vegetable stock
*1 cube unsalted vegetable bouillon
    (omit if using vegetable stock)*

dash of cayenne pepper
½ teaspoon white pepper
1 bay leaf

1 Melt margarine or butter in a saucepan and stir in rice. Cook over me-

dium-low heat, stirring constantly, 5
to 7 minutes.

2 Heat stock to a low boil.

3 Add simmering stock to rice. This mixture will boil furiously at first.

4 When the boiling and splattering has subsided, add remaining season-ings, cover, and cook approximately 45 minutes.

5 Allow rice to remain covered until served.

★

CURRIED BARLEY PILAF

YIELD: 6 SERVINGS

4½ cups chicken or vegetable stock
3 tablespoons unsalted margarine
  or butter
2 cups barley
4 cloves garlic

⅛ teaspoon cayenne pepper
½ teaspoon turmeric
4 tablespoons curry powder
few strands of saffron
1 cube unsalted vegetable bouillon

1 Bring stock to a simmer.

2 Melt margarine or butter in a large saucepan.

3 Add barley to margarine or butter and cook over low heat about 5 minutes. Stir often!

4 Mash and mince garlic and add to barley.

5 Stir barley and garlic together for a minute and add cayenne pepper, turmeric, curry powder, saffron, and bouillon cube.

6 Immediately add simmering stock. When mixture settles down to a simmer, cover and cook 25 minutes over medium-low heat.

★

SPANISH RICE

YIELD: 6 SERVINGS

2 cups cooked brown rice
  (see Basic Grains, page 121)
5 fresh red tomatoes
2 purple onions
4 cloves garlic

cayenne pepper to taste
2 tablespoons olive oil
1 teaspoon cumin
1 teaspoon white pepper
salt (optional)

1 Cook rice according to Basic Grains recipe, using chicken stock, not water.

2 Peel, core, seed, and chop tomatoes.

3 Sauté purple onions, garlic, and cayenne pepper in an iron skillet with olive oil.

4 Add chopped tomatoes and simmer 20 minutes.

5 Add cooked rice and simmer 10 to 15 minutes.

6 Add cumin, white pepper, and salt to taste during last few minutes of cooking.

★

LENTIL-GRAIN DUET

YIELD: 8 SERVINGS

*1 cup whole grain
  (barley, wheat, rye)*
2 cups lentils
8 cups unsalted stock or water
2 cups tomato juice

3 tablespoons margarine
1 tablespoon Worcestershire sauce
1 teaspoon white pepper
2 teaspoons cumin

1 Place grain and lentils in a pan and add stock or water to cover (about 6 cups).
2 Add tomato juice, then stir in remaining ingredients.
3 Cover and cook about 1 hour, adding stock or water from time to time. The grain and lentils should retain good texture. They should absorb the liquid and be dry (but not scorched) by the time they are served.
4 Fluff and serve.

★

BEAN AND RICE CREOLE CASSEROLE

A nutritious yet quick dish using precooked ingredients.

YIELD: 6 SERVINGS

*2 cups cooked beans (see Basic
  Beans, page 121)*
*2 cups cooked brown rice (see Basic
  Grains, page 121)*

*1½ cups Shrimp Creole sauce
  (page 165), shrimp omitted*
1 cup grated white cheese

1 Preheat oven to 400°.
2 Butter the sides and bottom of an 8-cup baking dish.
3 Combine beans, rice, and Creole sauce. Mix well and place into buttered baking dish.
4 Cover with aluminum foil and bake 35 minutes.
5 Remove casserole from oven and sprinkle evenly with grated cheese. Return to oven uncovered and bake 15 minutes more.
6 Remove from oven and allow to cool 10 to 15 minutes before serving.

★

POLENTA PIE

Mary Faulk Koock

YIELD: 4–6 SERVINGS

1 cup stone-ground yellow cornmeal
1 teaspoon sea salt (optional)
½ teaspoon crumbled dry sage
¼ teaspoon black pepper
3½ cups cold water
1 pound mild cheddar cheese, cubed
¼–½ cup chopped ripe olives

2 cloves garlic, minced
2 medium onions, chopped
½ cup chopped chile peppers
 (optional)
1 cup tomato sauce
1 tablespoon unrefined oil
1 tablespoon oregano

1 Preheat oven to 425°.
2 Mix cornmeal, sea salt, sage, and black pepper in a 2-quart saucepan.
3 Stir in cold water.
4 Cook, stirring constantly, until very thick. (This recipe does not lump.)
5 Pour into an oiled, flat 1½-quart baking dish.

6 Bake crust until firm, about 15 to 20 minutes, at 425°. Set aside.
7 Mix cheddar cheese, olives, garlic, onions, chile peppers, tomato sauce, oil, and oregano.
8 Spread over hot cornmeal crust and bake at 425° until cheese melts.

★

TOFU AMANDINE

YIELD: 4 SERVINGS AS SIDE DISH

½ cup unsalted margarine or butter
8 ounces tofu
½ teaspoon garlic powder
½ teaspoon paprika
¼ teaspoon cayenne pepper
¼ cup (scant) unbleached white flour

6 tablespoons slivered almonds
3 tablespoons lemon and/or lime juice
½ teaspoon white pepper
2 tablespoons freshly chopped green herb (parsley, basil, dill weed)
lemon or lime slices for garnish

1 Melt margarine or butter in a sauté pan.
2 Carefully cut tofu into rather thick strips, no larger than 1½ inches wide and 1 inch thick.
3 Combine garlic powder, paprika, cayenne pepper, and flour and spread mixture in a dish.
4 Gently coat tofu pieces in seasoned

flour mixture and place a single layer of tofu into a very lightly buttered baking dish.
5 Dribble about half of the melted margarine or butter on tofu and place under broiler for 12 minutes.
6 Meanwhile, sauté almonds in remaining margarine or butter.
7 When almonds are golden, remove

from heat. Stir in lemon or lime juice, white pepper, and chopped green herb.

8 When tofu is done, remove from broiler, place on serving platter, and pour almond mixture on top.

9 Serve immediately, garnished with lemon or lime slices and a sprig of the fresh herb you used with the almonds.

★

SKILLET-FRIED TOFU WITH JALAPEÑO PEPPERS

YIELD: 4 SERVINGS AS SIDE DISH

12 ounces tofu
5 tablespoons unbleached white flour
½ teaspoon cumin
3 tablespoons sesame oil

1 (or more) medium pickled jalapeño pepper, sliced
tamari soy sauce
lemon wedges

1 Slice tofu cakes crosswise into strips ½ inch thick and 2 inches long.

2 Combine flour and cumin and carefully roll tofu in the mixture.

3 Heat sesame oil in large iron skillet. Add tofu strips and fry until brown and crisp.

4 Quickly remove from heat and top each piece with a slice of jalapeño pepper.

5 Serve immediately with tamari soy sauce and lemon.

★

TEXAS TOFU TACOS

YIELD: 12 TACOS

18 ounces tofu
1 cup cooked cracked wheat (see Basic Grains, page 121)
½ cup cooked brown rice (see Basic Grains, page 121)
2 cloves garlic
1 small purple onion
½ teaspoon crushed red pepper
1 teaspoon whole cumin seed

3 tablespoons tomato paste
¼ cup extra virgin olive oil
12 whole wheat tortillas
½ cup grated Monterey Jack cheese
Guacamole (page 81)
Salsa Fresca (page 54)
Salsa Chipotle (page 55)
cilantro for garnish

1 Crumble tofu into a bowl with cracked wheat and brown rice.

2 Mince garlic and onion and add to tofu-grain mixture along with red pepper, cumin seed, and tomato paste.

3 Heat oil in a large skillet or wok and stir in tofu-grain mixture. Cook 3 to 4 minutes or until dish is thoroughly heated.

4 Heat tortillas Southwestern style by laying each one over a medium burner, either gas or electric, for just enough seconds to heat each side.

5 Serve tofu-grain taco mix and heated tortillas with grated cheese, guacamole, salsa fresca, and salsa chipotle, with sprigs of cilantro as a garnish.

CEREALS AND MIXES

GRANOLA CEREAL
YIELD: ABOUT 12 CUPS

½ pound rolled oats
½ pound soy flakes
½ pound wheat flakes
½ cup sunflower seeds
½ cup chopped almonds or walnuts
1 cup wheat bran

¼ cup safflower oil
½ cup honey or maple syrup
2 teaspoons vanilla extract
½ cup raisins
½ cup shredded coconut

1 Preheat oven to 300°.
2 Mix oats, soy and wheat flakes, sunflower seeds, nuts, and wheat bran.
3 In a saucepan, warm oil, honey or maple syrup, and vanilla, then combine with dry ingredients.
4 Bake on a baking sheet or shallow pan at 300° for 30 minutes. Stir occasionally.
5 When granola is cooked, remove from oven and add raisins and coconut.
6 Allow to cool thoroughly and seal in airtight container.

★

REDI-MIX

Our version of a really wonderful basic dry mix from Diet for a Small Planet.
Try it for breading instead of flour. See Diet for a Small Planet *for other uses.*
YIELD: ABOUT 6 CUPS

¾ cup unbleached whole flour
2½ cups whole wheat flour
¾ cup soy flour
1½ teaspoons salt (optional)

½ cup instant dry milk
*½ cup low-sodium baking powder
or ¼ cup regular baking powder*
1¼ cups wheat germ or bran

Mix thoroughly and store in a tightly covered jar in the refrigerator.

★

ITALIAN DRY MIX

This and the other complementary-protein dry mixes that follow are particularly useful for backpackers but are also good to have on hand for a tasty, healthful meal in a hurry. The finished dish is something between a casserole and a stew. Dry mixes can be stored up to 6 months.

YIELD: 4 SERVINGS

Ingredients to be soaked
¼ cup TVP (textured vegetable protein)
¼ cup corn grits
3 tablespoons split green peas
1 tablespoon dried crumbled tofu
2 tablespoons dried carrots
2 tablespoons dried minced onions
1 tablespoon dried mushrooms

Seasonings
2 tablespoons broken spinach pasta
2 tablespoons broken whole wheat pasta

2 teaspoons garlic granules
1 teaspoon oregano
1 teaspoon thyme
1 teaspoon basil
1 bay leaf
1 teaspoon black pepper
3 tablespoons dried tomato soup base
2 tablespoons Parmesan cheese

1 Mix together ingredients to be soaked and place in a plastic bag.
2 Mix together seasonings and place in a second plastic bag.
3 Store both bags together in a larger bag until needed. Be sure to mark bags clearly.

4 When ready to cook, place all ingredients to be soaked in 3 cups of water for 30 minutes.
5 Add seasonings, cover, and bring pot to simmer. Cook 35 to 40 minutes.

★

PROVENÇALE DRY MIX

YIELD: 4 SERVINGS

Ingredients to be soaked
¼ cup wheat flakes
¼ cup split red lentils
¼ cup TVP (textured vegetable protein)
¼ cup dried green beans

1 tablespoon dried minced onions
2 tablespoons dried chives

Seasonings
2 tablespoons chopped walnuts
3 tablespoons dried onion soup base

1 teaspoon garlic powder
1½ teaspoons ground, dried green
* peppercorns*
1 tablespoon tarragon

1 Mix together ingredients to be
soaked and place in a plastic bag.
2 Mix together seasonings and place
in a second plastic bag.
3 Store both bags together in a larger
bag until needed. Be sure to mark
bags clearly.

1 teaspoon thyme
1 tablespoon dried parsley
¼ teaspoon nutmeg

4 When ready to cook, place all ingredients to be soaked in 3 cups of
water for 30 minutes.
5 Add seasonings, cover, and bring
pot to simmer. Cook 35 to 40
minutes.

CURRY DRY MIX

YIELD: 4 SERVINGS

Ingredients to be soaked
6 tablespoons split red lentils
6 tablespoons brown Texmati rice
2 tablespoons dried minced onions
1 tablespoon dried carrots

Seasonings
¾ cup freeze-dried chicken
* (optional)*

2 tablespoons dried coconut
2 tablespoons pine nuts
2 tablespoons currants
1 tablespoon curry powder
2 teaspoons garam masala
few strands of saffron
¼ teaspoon cinnamon
½ teaspoon ground coriander seed
½ teaspoon crushed red pepper

1 Mix together ingredients to be
soaked and place in a plastic bag.
2 Mix together seasonings and place
in a second plastic bag.
3 Store both bags together in a larger
bag until needed. Be sure to mark
bags clearly.

4 When ready to cook, place all ingredients to be soaked in 3 cups of
water for 30 minutes.
5 Add seasonings, cover, and bring
pot to simmer. Cook 35 to 40
minutes.

★

MEXICAN DRY MIX

YIELD: 4 SERVINGS

Ingredients to be soaked
3 tablespoons mung beans
3 tablespoons barley
3 tablespoons brown Texmati rice

2 tablespoons millet
3 tablespoons TVP (textured
* vegetable protein)*
3 tablespoons dried minced onions

Seasonings

¹/₄ teaspoon crushed red pepper
1 teaspoon whole cumin seed
1 teaspoon ground cumin
2 teaspoons oregano
1 teaspoon thyme

1 tablespoon chili powder
1 teaspoon marjoram
*1 teaspoon coarsely ground black
  pepper*
*1 tablespoon dried tomato soup
  base*

1 Mix together ingredients to be soaked and place in a plastic bag.
2 Mix together seasonings and place in a second plastic bag.
3 Store both bags together in a larger bag until needed. Be sure to mark bags clearly.

4 When ready to cook, place all ingredients to be soaked in 3 cups of water for 30 minutes.
5 Add seasonings, cover, and bring pot to simmer. Cook 35 to 40 minutes.

★

CHICKEN AND HERB DRY MIX

YIELD: 4 SERVINGS

³/₄ cup freeze-dried chicken
¹/₄ cup couscous
*6 tablespoons freeze-dried cooked
  peas*
2 tablespoons dried chives
1 teaspoon dried minced onions
2 tablespoons sesame seeds
¹/₄ cup chopped nuts
¹/₂ teaspoon sage
¹/₈ teaspoon nutmeg

*1¹/₂ teaspoons coarsely ground black
  pepper*
¹/₂ teaspoon oregano
2 teaspoons thyme
1 teaspoon chervil
1 tablespoon dried parsley
1 teaspoon tarragon
¹/₂ teaspoon basil
¹/₂ teaspoon celery seed

1 Combine all ingredients and seal in a plastic bag until ready for use. Label bag.
2 To cook, bring 2¹/₂ cups water to a boil and add all ingredients.

3 Remove from heat, cover, and allow to stand 5 to 10 minutes.

PASTAS AND DUMPLINGS

★

BASIC PASTA

YIELD: 4 SERVINGS AS ENTRÉE

1 pound fresh pasta
4 quarts boiling water

1 Bring water to a rapid boil.
2 Drop pasta into water and stir gently to keep it from sticking.
3 Boil for about 3 minutes and test for tenderness. Do not overcook.

Dried pasta will take several minutes longer.
4 Drain, but do not rinse.
5 Serve immediately or incorporate into other dishes.

★

PASTA WITH PESTO

This dish is one of the glories of a summer herb garden. Pesto sauce should not be frozen for more than a few months. Fresh basil can, however, be pureed by itself and frozen until required.

YIELD: 6–8 SERVINGS

3 cups (loosely packed) whole fresh basil leaves or 1 1/2 cups pureed leaves
3/4 cup virgin olive oil
3/4 cup freshly grated Parmesan cheese
4 cloves garlic

2 tablespoons pine nuts
2 tablespoons lemon juice (optional)
1/2 cup unsalted margarine or butter
2 pounds fresh pasta (see Basic Pasta, page 132)

1 Combine all ingredients except margarine or butter and pasta in blender or food processor and puree until smooth.
2 Cook desired pasta, drain (reserving water), and toss with margarine or butter.

3 Add a spoonful or so of the hot pasta water to the pesto. Blend well and ladle sauce over fresh pasta.
4 Serve immediately with extra Parmesan cheese, or freeze.

★

PASTA PRIMAVERA
YIELD: 6 SERVINGS

1 purple onion
2 sweet red bell peppers
1 cup fresh asparagus tips
16–20 medium mushrooms (2 cups)
3 cloves garlic, minced
1 pound pasta
2 tablespoons unsalted margarine
  or butter
1 tablespoon olive oil
1 tablespoon paprika

cayenne pepper to taste
black pepper to taste
1 teaspoon oregano
½ teaspoon dill weed
¼ cup white wine
¼ cup cream
chopped green onion tops for
  garnish
6 tablespoons Parmesan cheese

1 Chop onion and bell peppers into large pieces (about 1 inch square). Slice off tips of asparagus. Quarter mushrooms. Mash and mince garlic.
2 Put 3 quarts of water on to heat. Proceed with rest of recipe until water comes to a boil, then add pasta and cook 3 to 5 minutes.
3 Melt margarine or butter with olive oil in a large sauté pan.
4 Add onion, bell peppers, and garlic and cook about 4 minutes.
5 Add mushrooms and asparagus tips and cook a few more minutes until tender.
6 Add paprika, cayenne and black pepper, oregano, dill weed, and white wine and cook 1 minute.
7 When pasta is cooked, drain and toss with cream and serve on a warm plate with vegetable mixture arranged around the edge. Garnish with chopped green onion tops. Sprinkle each serving with Parmesan cheese.

★

LINGUINE WITH MARCELLO SAUCE ARNO
Janice Beeson
YIELD: 4 SERVINGS

½ pound sweet Italian sausage
1 tablespoon cooking oil
3 cloves garlic, minced
¼ cup olive oil
½ pound mushrooms, quartered
6 tomatoes, peeled and chopped

2 teaspoons basil
9 2-inch-long strips of orange peel
  or 1 tablespoon chopped orange
  peel
salt and pepper to taste
cooked linguine for 4 servings

1 Slice sausage and sauté in cooking oil. Drain off oil and set sausage aside.
2 Sauté garlic in olive oil 3 minutes.
3 Add mushrooms and cook until slightly brown and moisture has evaporated.

4 Add tomatoes, basil, orange peel, salt, and pepper. Cook until moisture has evaporated.
5 Add sausage and cook until hot.
6 Serve over linguine.

★

NANNIE'S DUMPLINGS

YIELD: 6 SERVINGS

4 quarts Brown Poultry Stock (page 40) or water
1 3-pound chicken or rabbit
1³/₄ cups unbleached white flour
¹/₂ teaspoon salt

1 rounded tablespoon unsalted margarine or butter
¹/₂ cup low-fat milk
finely ground black pepper to taste

1 Bring stock or water to simmer and cook chicken or rabbit in it until tender (45 minutes to 1 hour).
2 Remove from heat and bone, cutting meat into bite-size pieces. Set meat aside until dumplings are cooked. Discard fat, skin, and bones.
3 Return stock to stove and bring to a low simmer.
4 To make dumplings, sift together flour and salt, then cut in margarine or butter, using a pastry blender. Stir in milk and form dough.

5 Roll dough out to ¹/₄ inch thick on floured surface. Cut into dumplings 1 inch wide and 2 inches long.
6 Drop dumplings separately and quickly into simmering stock. Simmer 3 to 5 minutes.
7 Add boned meat and cook another 5 minutes, stirring very gently. Test dumplings for doneness, season with black pepper, and serve immediately. Do not overcook or dumplings will disintegrate.

7

DAIRY PRODUCTS AND EGGS

★

CHILE CON QUESO
YIELD: 6 SERVINGS

3 cloves garlic
1 large purple onion
1 tablespoon olive oil
3 whole canned green chile peppers
or fresh green chile peppers,
roasted and peeled

½ teaspoon ground red pepper
½ teaspoon cumin
1 pound Monterey Jack cheese

1 Peel garlic and slice lengthwise into slivers.
2 Peel onion and slice into ⅛-inch rounds.
3 Seed whole canned green chiles or roast, peel, and seed fresh chiles (see *Chile Peppers*). Cut into strips.
4 Heat oil in a cast-iron skillet, add onions and garlic, and cook about 10 minutes over medium heat.

5 Add chiles, red pepper, and cumin and remove from heat.
6 Grate cheese and mix with other ingredients in a double boiler.
7 Simmer 15 or 20 minutes, stirring often, until cheese is thoroughly mixed and melted.
8 Serve immediately with warm tortillas or tortilla chips or it will begin to separate.

★

JALAPEÑO PIMIENTO CHEESE

This is an excellent way to use up all those bits of cheese that accumulate in the refrigerator.
YIELD: 8 – 10 SERVINGS

2 pounds assorted cheese
1 8-ounce jar chopped pimientos
6 pickled jalapeño peppers
¼ cup pickling vinegar from the can of peppers

¾ cup mayonnaise
½ teaspoon garlic powder

1 Grate cheese cold for easier work.
2 Drain pimientos and chop peppers.
3 Combine all ingredients.

4 Store covered in refrigerator. Serve as sandwich spread or stuffing for celery stalks.

★

COTTAGE CHEESE PATTIES

Susie Stover

YIELD: 6 SERVINGS

1 onion
1/2 green pepper
2 tablespoons unsalted margarine
  or butter
1 carrot
2 cups bread crumbs

2 cups low-fat cottage cheese
3 eggs
1 tablespoon prepared mustard
salt and pepper to taste
1/2 cup unbleached white flour
1/2 cup safflower oil (for frying)

1 Finely chop onion and green pepper and sauté 3 to 5 minutes in margarine or butter.
2 Grate carrot and combine with bread crumbs, cottage cheese, eggs, mustard, salt, and pepper.

3 Combine sautéed vegetables with cottage cheese mixture.
4 Mix and form into 12 flat patties.
5 Dust with flour and fry.

★

SCRAMBLED EGGS WITH TOFU

These protein breakfast foods are naturals with each other. A good introduction to tofu.

YIELD: 4 SERVINGS

6 whole eggs, minus 3 yolks
1/2 teaspoon tamari soy sauce
1/4 teaspoon white pepper
6 ounces tofu
3 medium green onions

3 tablespoons unsalted margarine
  or butter
4 teaspoons finely chopped fresh
  parsley
8 lemon wedges (1 whole lemon)

1 Whip eggs in a large mixing bowl.
2 Mix in tamari soy sauce and white pepper.
3 Crumble cake of tofu into egg mixture. Set aside.
4 Finely chop green onions.
5 Melt margarine or butter in a large cast-iron skillet. When it foams, add chopped green onion and sauté over medium heat about 1 minute.

6 Add egg-tofu mixture to skillet, but do not stir for 1 to 2 minutes. Then stir gently with wooden spoon until eggs and tofu are ready (soft or hard, as desired).
7 Chop fresh parsley, slice lemons, and garnish each serving with 1 teaspoon parsley and 2 lemon wedges.

★

BAKED OMELET (FRITTATA)

Good served with Tofu Mornay Sauce (page 51) in a bowl on the side.

Y I E L D : 4 S E R V I N G S

2 whole eggs
6 egg whites
1 teaspoon thyme
1 teaspoon tarragon

pinch of cayenne pepper
1 cup buttermilk
1 heaping teaspoon baking soda

1 Preheat oven to 350°.
2 Whip eggs and egg whites together with thyme, tarragon, and cayenne pepper.
3 Add buttermilk and baking soda.
4 Blend and pour into a buttered baking dish, approximately 7 by 12 inches.
5 Bake at 350° about 25 minutes.
6 Turn oven up to 450° for 2 or 3 minutes to brown the top, then serve.

★

CHEESE SOUFFLÉ

Ann Clark, La Bonne Cuisine School

———

The basic soufflé recipe of Austin's foremost French cooking school.

Y I E L D : 6 S E R V I N G S

5 tablespoons butter
3 tablespoons flour
1 cup milk
½ teaspoon salt
¼ teaspoon white pepper
pinch of cayenne pepper

4 egg yolks
1 cup grated Swiss cheese
5–6 egg whites (room temperature)
2–3 tablespoons grated Parmesan cheese

1 Preheat oven to 375°.
2 Melt 3 tablespoons butter in a saucepan and add flour. Cook until flour is lightly golden.
3 Heat milk and stir into roux.
4 Continue stirring over low heat until mixture has thickened. Add salt and pepper and remove from heat.
5 Beat egg yolks and dribble in a little of the hot milk mixture.
6 Mix well and add yolks to rest of hot milk mixture. Blend well.
7 Stir in ¾ cup grated Swiss cheese (reserve other ¼ cup for top of soufflé). Set aside.
8 In a separate bowl, beat egg whites until stiff and stir a third of the whites into cheese mixture.
9 Fold the rest of the egg whites into the soufflé batter and set aside.

10 Prepare a 6-cup soufflé dish by greasing bottom and sides with remaining 2 tablespoons butter and evenly coating with Parmesan cheese.

11 Turn soufflé batter into dish and top with remaining ¼ cup grated Swiss cheese.

12 Place in preheated oven and bake at 375° for 25 to 35 minutes.

★

SWEET POTATO PUDDING SOUFFLÉ

YIELD: 4 – 6 SERVINGS

3 medium sweet potatoes
3 tablespoons unsalted margarine
*   or butter*
2 tablespoons dark rum

1 tablespoon fructose
¼ teaspoon cinnamon
4 egg whites
pinch of salt

1 Wash and dry sweet potatoes, and rub each with about ½ teaspoon margarine or butter. Wrap in foil and bake at 375° until soft. Allow to cool.

2 Peel sweet potatoes and place in food processor with 3 tablespoons margarine or butter, dark rum, fructose, and cinnamon. Blend.

3 Rub a 5-cup soufflé mold with margarine or butter and dust with raw or brown sugar.

4 Beat egg whites (preferably in copper bowl reserved for that purpose) with pinch of salt until stiff peaks appear.

5 Add approximately one fourth of the egg whites to the sweet potato mixture and stir in, to lighten the mixture.

6 Carefully fold in the remaining egg whites.

7 Pour into the mold. Smooth the top. Using a teaspoon, scoop out a moat around the edge. Dollop scooped-out soufflé mixture onto the middle.

8 Place mold in pan containing enough water to come 1 or 2 inches up the side of the mold. Bake in pan of water at 375° for 40 to 45 minutes.

★

JALAPEÑO SPOON BREAD

A native Texas soufflé.

YIELD: 4 – 6 SERVING·S

3 tablespoons unsalted margarine
*   or butter*
1¼ cup yellow cornmeal
½ cup unbleached white flour

4 teaspoons low-sodium baking
*   powder or 2 teaspoons regular*
*   baking powder*
¼ teaspoon salt

2 whole eggs
1 egg white
1 cup buttermilk or yogurt

¼ cup chopped canned jalapeño peppers

1 Preheat oven to 400°. Grease a 6-cup soufflé mold or baking dish.
2 Melt margarine or butter and let cool slightly.
3 Stir together cornmeal, flour, baking powder, and salt.
4 Mix together eggs, egg white, buttermilk or yogurt, and melted margarine or butter. Combine with dry ingredients.
5 Add chopped jalapeño peppers and stir just until blended.
6 Pour into greased baking dish and bake at 400° for 35 minutes. Serve hot from the dish.

8

POULTRY, MEAT, AND SEAFOOD

POULTRY

★

BASIC GRILLED CHICKEN

1 Fifteen to 20 minutes before grill will be ready (see *Grilling*), put Pop Lowery's Barbecue Sauce (page 53) on stove to simmer.
2 Brush sauce on skin side of chicken.
3 Lay chicken skin side down on hottest areas of the grill.
4 Brush top side of chicken with sauce.
5 Turn every 7 to 8 minutes, brushing with sauce. Cooking will take at least 20 minutes.

★

HONEY-MADEIRA BRAISED CHICKEN

YIELD: 4 SERVINGS

2 *whole chicken breasts*
4 *green onions*
2 *tablespoons fresh grated and minced ginger*
4 *tablespoons sesame oil*
1/2 *cup Madeira wine*
3 *tablespoons honey*
2 *tablespoons tamari soy sauce*

1 Split, skin, and bone chicken breasts. Chop green onions and grate and mince ginger.
2 Heat oil in a skillet and add onion and ginger.
3 Stir over heat for a moment, and then add chicken breasts, turning until both sides are browned.
4 Combine Madeira wine, honey, and tamari soy sauce in a bowl.
5 Drain excess oil from skillet.
6 Pour wine mixture into skillet with chicken. Cover and simmer for 30 minutes.

★

LEMON-CUMIN BREAST OF CHICKEN

YIELD: 6 SERVINGS

3 *whole chicken breasts*
3 *tablespoons olive oil*
3 *lemons*
1/3 *cup dry white wine*
1 *teaspoon white pepper*
2 *teaspoons garlic powder*
2 *teaspoons cumin*

1 Split, skin, and bone chicken breasts, then pound them flat.
2 Line a deep baking dish with foil and brush bottom with 1 tablespoon olive oil.
3 Roll breasts in remaining olive oil and lay in the pan.
4 Squeeze lemons over chicken and pour on white wine.
5 Sprinkle generously with white pepper, garlic powder, and cumin.
6 Cover with waxed paper and marinate in the refrigerator at least 2 hours.
7 Broil approximately 7 minutes on each side, depending on size.

★

SAUTÉED CHICKEN BREASTS WITH ONION GRAVY

YIELD: 8 SERVINGS

4 whole chicken breasts
white pepper
2 tablespoons olive oil
3 purple onions
2 tablespoons unsalted margarine or butter

4 cups chicken stock
¼ cup drained canned green peppercorns
3 tablespoons flour
1 tablespoon Worcestershire sauce
tamari soy sauce to taste

1 Split, skin, and bone chicken breasts.
2 Sprinkle with white pepper.
3 Heat olive oil in a sauté pan and sauté chicken breasts over low heat until done.
4 Remove from pan and set aside on warm platter. Cover with foil.
5 Thinly slice purple onions.
6 Melt margarine or butter with olive oil in sauté pan used for chicken, then add onions. Cook until soft, stirring often.
7 While onions are cooking, heat stock to simmer.
8 Drain and slightly mash peppercorns. Add to onions and cook for a couple of minutes.
9 Add flour and cook 4 or 5 minutes longer, stirring constantly.
10 Add simmering stock.
11 Season with Worcestershire sauce and tamari soy sauce, and continue to simmer until gravy thickens.
12 Ladle gravy over warm chicken breasts and serve immediately.

★

SAUTÉED CHICKEN BREASTS WITH GREEN PEPPERCORN AND MUSTARD SAUCE

YIELD: 6 SERVINGS

3½ cups chicken stock
½ cup dry couscous
3 whole chicken breasts
1 teaspoon white pepper
3 tablespoons extra virgin olive oil

¼ cup drained canned green peppercorns
⅓ cup prepared French mustard
salt to taste

1 Heat ½ cup stock to boiling, remove from heat, add couscous, and cover. Allow to sit about 10 minutes.
2 Puree cooked couscous with 1¼ cup stock until very smooth and creamy.
3 Split, skin, and bone chicken breasts and sprinkle with white pepper.
4 Heat oil in a sauté pan large enough to hold all the chicken. Place chicken in pan and cook over moderately high heat 1 to 2 minutes.
5 Reduce heat and continue cooking. Turn chicken several times. Cook until light brown on both sides.
6 Remove from pan and set aside on a hot platter. Leave pan on low heat.
7 To simmering juices in sauté pan, add drained peppercorns. Stir around for a minute and add mustard.
8 When peppercorns and mustard have heated, add remaining 1¾ cup stock and blend.
9 Add couscous mixture to sauce and simmer for a few moments until it reaches the right consistency. Correct the seasoning.
10 Pour some of the sauce over platter of sautéed chicken and serve the rest on the side in a gravy boat.

★

SAUTÉED CHICKEN BREASTS WITH BRAISED JULIENNE OF VEGETABLES

YIELD: 6 SERVINGS

3 large whole chicken breasts
2 teaspoons white pepper
3 medium leeks
4 carrots
¼ cup very small julienne strips of ginger

3 tablespoons extra virgin olive oil
3 tablespoons unsalted margarine or butter
¼ teaspoon cayenne pepper
½ cup dry white wine

1 Split, skin, and bone chicken breasts. Season with white pepper and set aside.

2 Cut leeks into julienne strips and wash (see *Leeks*). Prepare julienne strips of carrots and ginger. You should have about 2 cups each of leeks and carrots.

3 Heat olive oil in one large sauté pan and margarine or butter in another.

4 To sauté pan containing margarine or butter, add leeks, carrots, ginger, cayenne pepper, and white wine. Cover and simmer over medium heat about 15 minutes, stirring 2 or 3 times during cooking.

5 As vegetables are braising, add chicken breasts to heated olive oil and turn until both sides are a nice light golden.

6 Serve chicken breast surrounded by a little ring of the vegetables, and pour a bit of the braising juice on the chicken. Serve immediately.

★

DOUBLE-DIPPED FRIED CHICKEN OR GAME BIRD

YIELD: 6 SERVINGS

3 whole chicken breasts
2 heaping cups unbleached white flour
2 teaspoons garlic powder
1 teaspoon white pepper
1 teaspoon thyme
1 teaspoon paprika

pinch of salt (optional)
3 cups yogurt
2½ cups Redi-Mix (page 128)
oil (1–1½ inches in pan)
Cream Gravy (page 50) or Tofu Béchamel (page 51)

1 Split, skin, and bone chicken breasts. Wipe lightly with damp towel.

2 In a paper or plastic bag, place unbleached white flour, garlic powder, white pepper, thyme, paprika, and salt.

3 Place chicken in the bag a few pieces at a time and shake.

4 Dip each piece of floured chicken in yogurt, roll in Redi-Mix, dip in yogurt again, and roll in Redi-Mix again.

5 Fry in 1 to 1½ inches of oil over high heat for 1 minute, then turn heat down to medium low to avoid burning the outside and undercooking the inside.

6 Cook the first side until deep golden brown, then turn chicken and cook the other side.

7 Drain on paper towels.

8 Serve immediately with cream gravy or béchamel sauce.

★

SOUTHERN FRIED CHICKEN

Liz Carpenter

YIELD: 4–6 SERVINGS

1 frying chicken (3–3½ pounds),
cut up
1 cup flour
1½ teaspoons salt (optional)

1½ teaspoons pepper
1 quart vegetable oil
Cream Gravy (page 50)

1 Soak cut-up chicken in 1 quart of cold water mixed with 1 tablespoon salt in a large bowl for 2 hours or longer.

2 Combine flour, salt, and pepper in a plastic or paper bag.

3 Remove chicken from water and pat dry with paper toweling. Add chicken to bag of flour, a few pieces at a time, and shake to coat well. As chicken is coated, place on a piece of waxed paper.

4 Pour enough oil in a large, deep skillet to fill it half full. (Oil must be deep enough to cover chicken.)

Heat oil until very hot (370° on deep-fat frying thermometer).

5 Add chicken, skin side down. When underside of chicken begins to brown, turn heat down to medium and partially cover with a lid.

6 Turn chicken after about 15 minutes or when completely browned on underside. Continue cooking, uncovered, until second side is browned. Drain thoroughly on paper toweling before serving. Keep warm in 250° oven while making gravy.

★

GREEN CHILE AND CHICKEN QUICHE

YIELD: 4 SERVINGS

6–8 whole canned green chile
peppers or fresh green Anaheim
chile peppers, roasted and peeled
2 whole chicken breasts
2 tablespoons olive oil
4 ounces tofu
¾ cup yogurt

2 whole eggs
2 egg whites
¼ teaspoon cayenne pepper
1 teaspoon cumin
1¼ cup grated Monterey Jack cheese
¼ cup grated yellow cheddar cheese

1 Preheat oven to 400°.

2 Seed whole canned green chiles or roast, peel, and seed green Anaheim chiles (see *Chile Peppers*).

3 Grease 10-inch pie pan with margarine or butter.

4 Line pie pan with chiles.

5 Split, skin, and bone chicken breasts,

dice, and sauté in olive oil. Remove from oil and set aside to cool.

6 Combine tofu, yogurt, whole eggs, egg whites, cayenne pepper, and cumin in food processor and puree.

7 Sprinkle Monterey Jack cheese into chile-lined pan.

8 Spread diced chicken over cheese.

9 Pour custard over all, and put grated cheddar cheese in the center.

10 Bake in preheated 400° oven 1 to 1¼ hours, or until knife inserted in center comes out clean.

11 Allow to set 10 to 15 minutes before serving.

★

TWO CHAMPAGNE CHICKENS IN A POT

YIELD: 6–8 SERVINGS

2 whole fresh chickens (about 3½ pounds each)
juice of 2 lemons
½ teaspoon white pepper
3 new potatoes
2 large carrots
2 turnips

3 purple onions
2 fresh ears of corn
2 oranges
6 whole garlic cloves
2 teaspoons thyme
1 split (small bottle) champagne
2 bay leaves

1 Preheat oven to 400°.

2 Trim away excess fat at cavity openings of chickens. Rinse chickens in cold water and pat dry.

3 Rub chickens inside and out with lemon juice and white pepper.

4 Cut new potatoes, carrots, onions, and turnips into large chunks. Chop ears of corn into about 8 pieces. Chop oranges into large chunks (do not peel). Peel garlic cloves and toss vegetables and oranges with garlic and thyme.

5 Stuff chickens with vegetable mixture. Place in Dutch oven and arrange remainder of vegetables around chickens.

6 Pour champagne over chicken and vegetables.

7 Top each chicken with a bay leaf.

8 Cover and bake at 400° for 2½ to 3 hours.

9 Conserve liquid and serve with chicken.

★

ROAST BREAST OF TURKEY

There is no reason to wait until holidays to enjoy this all-American bird. To serve roast turkey for an everyday meal, purchase and cook only the breast section. Four- to 5-pound turkey breasts are available year-round in groceries and supermarkets.

YIELD: 6 – 8 SERVINGS

2 stalks celery
1 carrot
1 purple onion
4½ pounds breast of turkey
1 teaspoon coarsely ground black
  pepper
1 teaspoon sage

1 teaspoon thyme
4 or 5 bay leaves, crushed
½ cup unsalted margarine or butter
1¾ cups Brown Poultry Stock
  (page 40)
juice of ½ orange
Brown Gravy (recipe follows)

1 Preheat oven to 325°.
2 Chop celery and carrot, and slice purple onion.
3 Sprinkle chopped vegetables onto the bottom of a roasting pan to form a bed on which the turkey will roast.
4 Wipe the turkey breast clean with a damp cloth and sprinkle the cavity with black pepper, sage, and thyme.
5 Place seasoned breast skin side up on vegetable bed in roasting pan. Sprinkle bay leaves around the edges.

6 Simmer together margarine or butter, brown poultry stock, and orange juice.
7 Very generously baste turkey breast with stock mixture. Save rest of mixture for basting during cooking.
8 Place uncovered roasting pan into 325° oven and cook 3 hours, basting every 15 to 20 minutes until basting liquid is all used. Then continue basting with drippings in roasting pan.
9 When done, remove from oven, slice, and serve with brown gravy.

★

BROWN GRAVY

YIELD: 4 CUPS

4 cups stock
4 tablespoons fat from pan

3 tablespoons flour
salt and pepper

1 Heat stock to simmer.
2 Add flour to fat in skillet and cook until lightly browned.
3 Add heated stock and simmer, stir-

ring constantly, until gravy reaches desired consistency. Season with a bit of salt and pepper if desired.

★

POULTRY DRESSING

Pearl Dean

YIELD: 10–12 SERVINGS

¼–½ cup poultry stock or water
8 cups chopped celery
4 cups chopped green onions
1 cup chopped parsley
1 pan cornbread (9-by-11½-inch pan)
1 small loaf white bread, toasted crisp

1 cup unsalted margarine or butter
6 eggs
2 teaspoons thyme
3 tablespoons sage
salt and pepper to taste

1 Preheat oven to 350°.
2 Heat stock or water to simmering.
3 Chop celery, onions, and parsley.
4 Crumble cornbread and toast in large bowl. Moisten with stock or hot water.
5 Melt margarine or butter in heavy skillet, add celery, onions, and parsley, and sauté until light amber in color.

6 Add sautéed vegetables to bread; add eggs, thyme, sage, salt, and pepper, and mix well.
7 Bake in large pan or roaster at 350° for 2½ to 3 hours. After the first hour of baking, stir and scrape sides and bottom every 30 minutes.
8 Add extra stock or water if dressing gets too dry.

★

ROAST CHICKEN STUFFED WITH APRICOTS, APPLES, AND RAISINS

Sarah Sutton

YIELD: 4–6 SERVINGS

½ pound dried apricots
1 large chicken (at least 4 pounds)
1 onion, chopped
4–6 tablespoons unsalted margarine or butter
2 medium apples

½ cup seedless raisins
1 teaspoon cinnamon
salt and pepper to taste
1 teaspoon allspice
1 teaspoon poultry seasoning

1 Soak dried apricots in water 1 to 2 hours.
2 Heat oven to 350°.
3 Wash chicken and pat dry.

4 Chop onion and sauté in 2 or 3 tablespoons margarine or butter until transparent.

5 Drain and chop apricots. Peel, core, and chop apples.
6 Combine apricots, apples, and raisins, add to sautéed onions, and cook 2 to 3 minutes. Season with cinnamon and salt and pepper to taste.
7 Stuff chicken with sautéed onion-fruit mixture.

8 Season outside of chicken with all-spice, poultry seasoning, and more pepper if desired.
9 Roast chicken uncovered at 350° about 1½ hours. After the first 20 minutes, dot the top of the chicken with 2 or 3 tablespoons margarine or butter, and cover with foil for remaining cooking time.

★

GARLIC-GRILLED CHICKEN, ONIONS, AND TOMATOES

YIELD: 6 SERVINGS

3 whole chicken breasts
6 small purple onions
6 small tomatoes (not cherry)
5 cloves garlic

2 tablespoons coarsely ground black pepper
¼ cup extra virgin olive oil

1 Prepare charcoal and grill (see *Grilling*).
2 Split, skin, and bone chicken breasts.
3 Slice off both ends of onions and peel off outside layers. Slice off tops and bottoms of tomatoes.
4 Place chicken, onions, and tomatoes in a large, shallow dish or

bowl and sprinkle with black pepper.
5 Turn on blender and add peeled garlic cloves and oil.
6 Baste chicken, onions, and tomatoes with garlic and oil.
7 Grill all 3 things at once and serve immediately.

★

GRILLED CHICKEN FINGERS

Delicious served with grilled vegetables.

YIELD: 4–6 SERVINGS

3 whole chicken breasts
1 cup beer
¼ cup Salsa Chipotle (page 55)

2 tablespoons Worcestershire sauce
2 teaspoons coarsely ground black pepper

1 Split, skin, and bone chicken breasts. Cut meat into long strips about ½

inch wide. Place in deep glass dish or bowl and set aside.

2 Combine beer, salsa chipotle, Worcestershire sauce, and black pepper. Blend well and pour onto chicken fingers. Cover and marinate in refrigerator 2 to 3 hours.

3 Prepare grill (see *Grilling*) and grill chicken fingers.

BASIC SMOKED POULTRY

poultry
finely ground black pepper

1 quart boiling water
1 whole pod fresh garlic

1 Wipe the poultry to be smoked with a damp cloth. Sprinkle each piece with black pepper and arrange on smoking racks.
2 Separate individual garlic cloves from whole garlic pod and roughly crush each with the side of a knife (it is not necessary to peel them).
3 Bring water to a boil and pour into smoker pan.
4 Place crushed garlic into smoker pan with water, and put the racks of poultry into position.
5 Securely cover smoker and allow

poultry to smoke the required length of time. Add water if necessary. Turn poultry once during cooking.

Smoking Time
whole chicken: 4 hours
cut-up chicken: 2 hours
turkey or goose: 50 minutes per pound
Cornish game hens: 2 hours
duckling: 4 hours
quail: 1½ hours
pheasant: 2¾ hours

HERB-SMOKED TURKEY

Donald Wertz

Goose or duck may be used also; adjust the stuffing quantities accordingly.

YIELD: 14–18 SERVINGS

1 whole turkey (12–14 pounds)
2 quarts rich sauerkraut juice
2–3 yellow onions
2–3 sweet apples
3 stalks celery
3 stalks fresh rosemary or 1 tablespoon dried, crushed rosemary

4 sprigs fresh sage or 1 tablespoon dried sage
10 sprigs fresh thyme or 2 tablespoons dried thyme

1 Wash and dry turkey.

2 Bring sauerkraut juice to a boil; keep hot.

3 Peel onions and cut into quarters. Peel and core apples and cut into quarters. Chop celery and fresh herbs.

4 Stuff cavity of bird with onion, apples, celery, and fresh herbs. If using dried herbs, sprinkle them inside the cavity, then stuff with onions, apples, and celery.

5 Set bird on smoker rack.

6 Carefully pour 1 quart hot sauerkraut juice into smoker pan.

7 Set prepared bird into smoker; close lid. If coals are hot enough, bird should cook to well done in 50 minutes per pound. Replenish hot sauerkraut juice every 1½ hours. If sauerkraut juice runs out, use hot water.

★

LEMON-BASIL SMOKED CHICKEN

Donald Wertz

YIELD: 4 – 6 SERVINGS

2 quarts water
½ cup fresh lemon juice
6 tablespoons dried basil
2 stalks celery
2 yellow onions
1 whole chicken (3 – 4 pounds)

black pepper
6 strips bacon (use high-quality,
thick-sliced, smokehouse-cured
bacon; thin commercial bacon
will shrivel excessively)

1 Bring water to a boil; add lemon juice and basil.

2 Wash and string celery stalks and chop. Peel onions and cut into quarters.

3 Wash and dry chicken.

4 Sprinkle cavity of chicken with black pepper.

5 Stuff chicken with celery and onion and place on smoker rack.

6 Cover as much of the bird as possible with strips of bacon. This will both flavor it and keep it from drying out. Fasten bacon strips with toothpicks where necessary to prevent them from falling off.

7 Carefully pour 1 quart lemon-basil tea into smoker pan.

8 Place prepared bird into smoker; close lid. If coals are hot enough, chicken should cook to well done in 45 minutes per pound. Replenish hot lemon-basil tea every 1½ hours. If tea runs out, use hot water.

Variation

1 Make a paste of margarine or butter, basil, and lemon.

2 Carefully loosen skin of chicken and stuff paste in between skin and meat.

3 Pour hot dry white wine into the smoker pan.

MEAT

★

FEGATO ALLA ARNO

Janice Beeson

YIELD: 4 SERVINGS

4 pounds calf or veal liver
1 cup flour
2 tablespoons unsalted margarine
*　or butter*

1 small onion
½ cup Madeira wine
½ teaspoon sage
salt and pepper to taste

1 Trim any fat and membrane from liver. Pat dry.
2 Dip each side in flour and shake off excess, leaving very little flour on the meat.
3 Melt margarine or butter in skillet and brown liver quickly. Remove from skillet.
4 Cut onion into thin slices and sauté

in same pan (add more margarine or butter if necessary) until golden.
5 Stir in Madeira wine.
6 Add sage, salt, and pepper. Reduce to desired consistency. Return liver to pan just until hot. Liver should be pink in the middle.
7 Spoon sauce and onions over meat and serve hot.

★

GRILLED RIBEYE OF VEAL

YIELD: 4–6 SERVINGS

2½ pounds ribeye of veal
2 tablespoons olive oil

3 cloves garlic
freshly ground black pepper

1 Prepare grill (see *Grilling*).
2 Rub ribeye of veal with very light coating of olive oil.
3 Cut each clove of garlic into several slivers.
4 Stud meat with slivers of garlic.

5 Grill approximately 6 minutes per pound for medium-done meat with a warm pink center.
6 Serve with Fresh Herb Butter (page 44) or alone.

★

ROAST VEAL WITH VEGETABLE SAUCE

YIELD: 10 – 14 SERVINGS

*10 tablespoons unsalted margarine
  or butter*
4 pounds top round veal roast
freshly ground black pepper
1 onion
2 leeks
3 stalks celery
2 carrots
4 cloves garlic

1 teaspoon thyme
5 bay leaves
5 sprigs fresh rosemary
1 cup dry red wine
*2 tablespoons unbleached white
  flour*
2 cups chicken stock
*fresh rosemary and parsley for
  garnish*

1 Melt 8 tablespoons (1 stick) margarine or butter.

2 Rub roast with melted margarine or butter and sprinkle with plenty of black pepper.

3 Place roast in a roasting pan or baking dish and cook uncovered for 1 hour at 400°.

4 While meat is roasting, coarsely chop onion, leeks, celery, and carrots. Slice garlic.

5 Remove roasted meat from oven. Turn it over and sprinkle vegetables, garlic, and thyme on top and around the bottom. Place a bay leaf and a rosemary sprig at sides and ends of roast and on top.

6 Return roast to oven and roast uncovered another 20 to 30 minutes, or until vegetables are wilted and beginning to brown.

7 Remove from oven and pour red wine over meat. Cover with foil and cook about 20 minutes more.

8 Remove roast from pan, wrap in foil, and set in a warm place.

9 Remove herbs from pan and discard. With a wooden spoon, stir vegetables and liquid around in roasting pan. (Red wine added earlier will naturally deglaze pan.) Pour mixture into a food processor and puree until very smooth.

10 Heat chicken stock to a simmer.

11 Melt remaining 2 tablespoons margarine or butter and stir in flour, cooking until golden brown. Add simmering chicken stock and continue to simmer about 5 minutes.

12 Stir vegetable puree into simmering stock and continue to cook over low heat. Stir sauce often and simmer until it reaches the desired consistency. Taste and correct seasoning.

13 Slice meat and arrange on a warmed platter. Ladle some of sauce over meat and garnish with fresh herbs. Serve extra sauce in a gravy boat.

★

BROILED VEAL CUTLETS WITH MANGO

YIELD: 4–6 SERVINGS

1½ cups wheat bran
3 teaspoons garlic powder
1 teaspoon thyme
½ teaspoon cayenne pepper
3 pounds veal cutlets

2 tablespoons unsalted margarine
 or butter, melted
3–4 ripe mangoes
lemon wedges for garnish

1 Combine wheat bran, garlic powder, thyme, and cayenne pepper. Place this mixture in a low-sided pan or dish and dredge veal cutlets in it.
2 Arrange breaded veal cutlets in a single layer in a large baking dish or dishes.
3 Place under broiler and broil about 10 minutes.
4 While cutlets are broiling, melt

margarine or butter. Peel mangoes and slice into wedges. Dip wedges in melted margarine or butter.
5 After 10 minutes of broiling, remove cutlets from broiler and turn them over. Arrange mango slices around and in between pieces of meat.
6 Broil cutlets and mangoes 12 minutes. Serve immediately with lemon wedges as garnish.

★

ROAST RIBEYE

YIELD: 6–8 SERVINGS

2 tablespoons olive oil
3 pounds boned ribeye roast
1 teaspoon white pepper

1 teaspoon pureed garlic
½ cup water

1 Preheat oven to 400°.
2 Heat olive oil in large frying pan over medium heat.
3 Sear meat on all sides. Remove from pan and cool slightly.
4 Rub meat with a paste made from white pepper and pureed garlic.

5 Place on rack in uncovered roasting pan and add water to pan.
6 Place on middle rack of oven and immediately turn oven down to 350°.
7 Roast 1½ to 2 hours, depending on degree of doneness desired.

★

CHICKEN-FRIED STEAK

YIELD: 6 SERVINGS

3 pounds round steak, cube steak, or veal cutlet
2 cups unbleached white flour
3 teaspoons paprika
3 teaspoons garlic powder
3 teaspoons finely ground black pepper
¾ teaspoon cumin
2 eggs
1 cup milk
3 cups Redi-Mix (page 128)
cooking oil (1 inch deep in frying pan)
Cream Gravy (page 50)

1 Trim fat and gristle from meat and cut into serving pieces.
2 In a shallow dish, combine flour, 1 teaspoon each paprika, garlic powder, and black pepper, and ¼ teaspoon cumin.
3 Beat eggs in a bowl and add milk. Combine with 1 teaspoon each paprika, garlic powder, and black pepper, and ¼ teaspoon cumin.
4 In another shallow dish combine Redi-Mix, 1 teaspoon each paprika, garlic powder, and black pepper, and ¼ teaspoon cumin.
5 Dredge each piece of meat in seasoned flour, shake off excess, and dip into milk-egg mixture, then roll in seasoned Redi-Mix. Set aside on pieces of waxed paper until all pieces of meat have been prepared.
6 Heat oil to medium high and cook meat in several batches, turning until both sides are a deep golden brown. Avoid overcooking the breading.
7 Drain on paper towels and set aside on a warm platter. Serve immediately with cream gravy.

★

FAJITAS

YIELD: 6 SERVINGS

3 pounds flank steak
½ teaspoon oregano
1 teaspoon garlic powder
1 teaspoon chili powder
1 teaspoon or more Tabasco sauce
1 teaspoon ground coriander seed
1 tablespoon cumin
2 tablespoons Worcestershire sauce
1 tablespoon cracked black pepper
1 cup dry red wine

1 Combine all ingredients except flank steak.
2 Marinate flank steak in this mixture at least 2 hours.
3 Grill meat, basting with marinade, until cooked to taste (see Grilling).
4 Remove meat from grill. Slice on the bias in very thin strips.
5 Serve immediately with:

hot flour or whole-wheat tortillas
Guacamole (page 81)
chopped tomatoes
chopped onions
shredded lettuce

grated cheese
sour cream or Mock Sour Cream
   (page 89)
a variety of salsas

★

R O A S T   V E N I S O N

Ralph Gilster

YIELD: 6–8 SERVINGS

3 pounds backstrap or other roast
   of venison
coarsely ground black pepper

Marinade
1 quart dry red wine
3 large onions
3 bay leaves
6 cloves garlic
½ cup lemon juice
8 cloves

½ cup gin
1 tablespoon prepared horseradish
1 tablespoon molasses
1 teaspoon tarragon
1 teaspoon basil
1 bottle Italian salad dressing

several slices of bacon
4 medium potatoes
4 large carrots
⅓ cup unbleached white flour

1 Rub roast with coarsely ground
  black pepper.
2 Prepare marinade by combining
  marinade ingredients.
3 Pour mixture over venison and
  marinate at least 12 hours, longer if
  possible.
4 Preheat oven to 350°.
5 Remove venison from marinade.
  Strain marinade and reserve for
  later use. Wrap venison with bacon
  for easy larding.
6 Slice potatoes and carrots and place

around bacon-wrapped roast in a
roasting pan. Roast in 350° oven
1½ to 2 hours.
7 Remove roasted potatoes and carrots and arrange on a warm serving
  platter.
8 Stir flour into ⅓ cup drippings over
  low heat and cook until flour is
  golden brown.
9 Pour in strained marinade. Stir until
  thickened and serve as sauce over
  venison.

★

MINT-SMOKED LAMB

Donald Wertz

YIELD: 4–6 SERVINGS

2 quarts spearmint tea
1 leg of lamb
several cloves garlic
½ cup flour

1 teaspoon black pepper
1 teaspoon tarragon
1 teaspoon thyme
¼ cup olive oil

1 Make 2 quarts of strong spearmint tea; keep hot.
2 Rinse lamb; pat dry.
3 Make several slits around lamb and insert a peeled garlic clove into each.
4 Combine flour, black pepper, tarragon, and thyme and dredge leg of lamb in seasoned flour.
5 Sear on all sides in hot olive oil.
6 Remove meat from skillet; set on smoker rack.

7 Pour hot mint tea into smoker pan, being careful not to splash any on the coals.
8 Set prepared lamb into smoker; close lid. If the coals are hot enough, the lamb should take about 45 minutes per pound to cook (medium rare). You should not have to open the smoker except to replenish the pan with hot tea every 1½ hours. If tea runs out, use hot water.

★

FRUIT-SMOKED PORK ROAST

Donald Wertz

YIELD: 8–10 SERVINGS

2 quarts hot water
4 pounds pork roast
½ cup flour
1 teaspoon black pepper
1 teaspoon ground ginger
1 teaspoon powdered orange peel

¼ cup olive oil
2 medium yellow onions, quartered
3 handfuls dried apples
2 handfuls dried currants
1 handful dried apricots

1 Boil water; keep hot.
2 Rinse pork roast; pat dry.
3 Combine flour, black pepper, ginger, and orange peel and dredge pork roast in seasoned flour.
4 Sear on all sides in hot olive oil.

5 Remove from skillet; set on smoker rack.
6 Pour small amount of hot water into smoker pan. Add quartered onions and dried fruit. Carefully fill the pan with more hot water.

7 Set prepared pork roast into smoker; close lid. If coals are hot enough, the pork should cook to well done in 1 hour per pound. Add hot water to smoker pan every hour or so. Be sure fruit does not get dry or it will char.

SEAFOOD

★

OYSTERS FIORENTINA ARNO

Janice Beeson

YIELD: 4 SERVINGS

2 packages frozen leaf spinach
1 tablespoon unsalted margarine or
  butter
¾ cup chopped onion
½ cup Béchamel Sauce (page 50)
1½ ounces licorice liqueur

salt and pepper to taste
32–48 shelled oysters
½ cup grated Parmesan cheese
1 cup cooked, crumbled bacon
lemon slices for garnish

1 Preheat oven to 400°.
2 Cook spinach. Drain, wrap in towel, wring out all moisture, and chop.
3 Melt margarine or butter in large sauté pan and sauté chopped onion until transparent.
4 Add spinach, béchamel sauce, liqueur, salt, and pepper. Cook 5 minutes.
5 Divide spinach mixture onto 4 ovenproof plates and place 8 to 12 drained oysters on top of spinach on each plate.
6 Sprinkle with Parmesan cheese and bacon.
7 Bake in 400° oven until edges of oysters curl.
8 Garnish with lemon slices and serve immediately.

★

GINGERED SCALLOP AND OYSTER STEW

YIELD: 6 SERVINGS

2 tablespoons tiny julienne of fresh
  ginger
3 tablespoons unsalted margarine
  or butter
6 cups low-fat milk
1 pound scallops (including liquor
  or juice)

1 pound oysters (including liquor or
  juice)
salt and freshly ground black pepper
  to taste

1 Peel fresh ginger root. Slice very thinly and cut into tiny slivers.
2 In a large skillet or soup pan melt margarine or butter over medium heat until it begins to foam slightly.
3 Add ginger to foaming butter. Cook

1 to 2 minutes, stirring constantly, until ginger is just tender. Be careful not to overcook, as it will brown and crisp quickly.

4 Remove pan from heat and stir in milk. Bring to low simmer.

5 While soup is coming to a simmer, remove the small tough muscle from each scallop, if necessary. (Muscle pieces may be used to make stock or as a treat for the kitties.)

6 Add prepared scallops, along with their liquor, to soup as soon as it simmers.

7 Simmer scallops gently 1 to 2 minutes, then add fresh oysters, including their liquor.

8 Finish stew by simmering and stirring another 2 minutes.

9 Ladle into warmed soup bowls. Allow each guest to season with salt and fresh black pepper.

★

SINGING SHRIMP

Our version of a recipe that derives ultimately from one served at Brennan's in New Orleans.

YIELD: 6–8 SERVINGS

1 bunch green onions
5 cloves garlic
4 tablespoons unsalted margarine
or butter
2 tablespoons olive oil
4 pounds cleaned, peeled, deveined
small shrimp

juice of 1 lemon
freshly grated black pepper
¼ teaspoon ground cloves
¾ cup dry white wine

1 Slice green onion into small rounds and mash garlic.

2 Melt margarine or butter and blend in olive oil; heat.

3 Sauté onion and garlic in margarine or butter and oil 1 or 2 minutes.

4 Add shrimp; stir and sauté 4 to 6 minutes, until they *begin* to turn white. Important: The shrimp are done when they turn white (after 7 to 10 minutes). Proceed to step 5

before this happens. Do not overcook.

5 Add to shrimp during the last 2 or 3 minutes of cooking: lemon juice, generous grating of fresh black pepper, ground cloves.

6 At the last moment, turn the heat very high and add dry white wine. The sizzling of the wine is the "singing." Serve over rice.

★

SHRIMP CREOLE

YIELD: 6–8 SERVINGS

¼ cup flour
2 tablespoons safflower oil
2 tablespoons extra virgin olive oil
1 cup chopped purple onion
½ cup chopped green onion
½ cup chopped celery
½ cup chopped bell pepper
5 cloves garlic, minced
1 large can stewed tomatoes

1 small can tomato paste
6 cups chicken or turkey stock
1 teaspoon red pepper
¼ teaspoon ground cloves
¼ teaspoon allspice
1 tablespoon chopped fresh basil
3 pounds cleaned, peeled, deveined
*   shrimp*
Brown Rice Pilaf (page 122)

1 Make a roux in a large cast-iron Dutch oven with flour, safflower oil, and olive oil. Simmer over a low flame until deep golden brown, stirring very frequently.
2 Add purple and green onions, celery, bell pepper, and garlic to roux. Cook until vegetables are soft.

3 Add tomatoes and tomato paste and cook about 10 minutes.
4 Add stock and seasonings and cook 45 minutes at low simmer.
5 Add shrimp and simmer 10 to 15 minutes until shrimp are cooked but not overdone.
6 Serve over brown rice pilaf.

★

CORNMEAL-FRIED SHRIMP

YIELD: 4–6 SERVINGS

2 pounds jumbo or large shrimp
1½ cups unbleached white flour
3 teaspoons garlic powder
3 teaspoons white pepper
2 cups low-fat yogurt
1 tablespoon paprika

dash of Tabasco sauce
3 cups yellow cornmeal
4 cups light cooking oil
lemon wedges
Seafood Cocktail Sauce (page 52)

1 Peel and devein shrimp, leaving tail section intact (see *Shrimp*). Place on ice and reserve in refrigerator until other ingredients are prepared.
2 Combine flour with 1 teaspoon each garlic powder and white pepper in a paper bag, and shake well to mix. Set aside.

3 In a mixing bowl, combine yogurt, 1 teaspoon each garlic powder and white pepper, paprika, and Tabasco sauce. Mix well with a whisk and set aside.
4 In a shallow baking dish or platter, combine cornmeal and 1 teaspoon each garlic powder and white pepper. Stir well with a fork and set

aside with flour and yogurt mixtures.

5 Heat oil in a deep cast-iron skillet.

6 While oil is heating, arrange from left to right: flour, yogurt, cornmeal, and a large piece of waxed paper.

7 Place shrimp in paper bag with flour and shake until all pieces of shrimp are coated with flour.

8 Remove shrimp one by one and shake off excess flour. Dip into yogurt, roll in cornmeal, and arrange on waxed paper.

9 When all of shrimp has been breaded and oil is hot, begin to cook in batches of 8 to 12, depending on size of pan. Place each batch on a warm platter until all are cooked. Serve immediately with lemon wedges and cocktail sauce.

★

SHRIMP IN PAPRIKA SAUCE WITH PASTA PRIMAVERA

YIELD: 6 SERVINGS

3 pounds large shrimp
2 sweet red bell peppers
1 purple onion
1 cup asparagus tips
16–20 medium-sized mushrooms (2 cups)
3 cloves garlic
1 pound fresh pasta
11 tablespoons unsalted margarine or butter
2 tablespoons extra virgin olive oil

4 tablespoons paprika
1 tablespoon Worcestershire sauce
cayenne pepper to taste
black pepper to taste
1 teaspoon oregano
½ teaspoon dill weed
¼ cup white wine
¼ cup cream
chopped green onion tops for garnish
grated Parmesan cheese for garnish

1 Peel, devein, and butterfly shrimp (see *Shrimp*) and reserve on ice.

2 Chop bell peppers and onion into approximately 1-inch-square pieces. Chop off tips of asparagus, quarter mushrooms, and mash and mince garlic.

3 Bring 3 quarts of water to a boil and begin cooking pasta.

4 Heat 2 tablespoons margarine or butter and 1 tablespoon olive oil in a large sauté pan and add onions, peppers, and garlic.

5 Cook 3 to 4 minutes, stirring often.

6 Add mushrooms and asparagus tops and cook until tender.

7 While vegetables are cooking, heat 6 tablespoons margarine or butter and 1 tablespoon olive oil in a second skillet and sauté shrimp on one side.

8 Sprinkle 2 tablespoons paprika into the pan and turn the shrimp. Add remaining paprika, Worcestershire sauce, cayenne pepper, black pepper, oregano, and dill weed.

9 Cook about 2 minutes or until shrimp is almost done, then add white wine.

10 Sizzle shrimp for a moment. Cover and remove from heat.

11 Remove vegetables from heat.

12 Remove pasta from boiling water and toss in a preheated bowl with remaining 3 tablespoons margarine or butter and cooked vegetables.

13 Mound a serving of pasta and vegetable mixture in the middle of a plate and surround with 6 to 8 shrimp. Place plates in a warm place.

14 Add cream to contents of pan shrimp was cooked in and heat until somewhat reduced. Pour a bit of liquid on each mound of pasta.

15 Top with chopped green onion tops and serve immediately with a bowl of Parmesan cheese to be passed.

★

BAKED SHRIMP AND EGGPLANT

YIELD: 8 SERVINGS

*3 cups chopped raw shrimp
(about 2 pounds)*
2 large eggplants
*³/₄ cup chopped green onions
(4 or 5)*
*¹/₂ cup chopped green pepper
(1 medium)*
4 cloves garlic
2 tablespoons extra virgin olive oil
1 tablespoon unbleached white flour
*1 cup chopped fresh tomatoes
(2–3 medium)*
¹/₄ cup tomato paste
¹/₂ cup chopped pimientos
1 tablespoon chopped parsley

2 tablespoons paprika
*2 teaspoons coarsely ground black
pepper*
¹/₄ teaspoon cayenne pepper
*1 tablespoon lemon juice (about ¹/₂
lemon)*
¹/₄ teaspoon cloves
¹/₄ teaspoon allspice
1 teaspoon thyme
¹/₂ teaspoon fructose
1 teaspoon Worcestershire sauce
1 whole egg
1 egg white
1¹/₂ cups bread crumbs

1 Preheat oven to 300°.

2 Peel, devein, and chop shrimp (see *Shrimp*). Place on ice and set in refrigerator.

3 Wash and remove stems from eggplants and immerse in boiling water 12 to 15 minutes.

4 Cut eggplants in half lengthwise and scoop out pulp. Be careful not to tear eggplant shell, which should be very thin. Set both pulp and peel aside.

5 Chop green onions and green pepper, and mince garlic.

6 Heat olive oil in a large skillet and sauté green onions, green pepper, and garlic 5 minutes.

7 Add flour and stir for 3 minutes.

8 Peel, juice, seed, and chop tomatoes.

9 Add chopped tomatoes to skillet along with tomato paste, chopped pimientos, chopped parsley, paprika, black pepper, cayenne pepper, lemon juice, cloves, allspice, thyme, fructose, and Worcestershire sauce.

10 Cook 3 minutes, then add shrimp. Continue cooking, stirring frequently, until shrimp is almost cooked, about 4 or 5 minutes.

11 Remove from heat and allow to cool slightly.

12 While mixture is cooling, oil a 2-quart soufflé dish or other deep baking dish and line with reserved eggplant peel, leaving enough hanging over the edges to be folded over the top of the dish later.

13 Beat together egg and egg white and add about ½ cup of the hot shrimp mixture, a tablespoonful at a time. Return egg and shrimp mixture to the rest of shrimp stuffing.

14 Chop reserved eggplant pulp and stir into shrimp mixture along with bread crumbs. Mix well and turn into eggplant-lined baking dish. Fold pieces of eggplant over top of dish and bake at 300° for 45 minutes.

15 Remove from oven and allow to stand 5 to 10 minutes. Turn baked shrimp and eggplant out of pan onto a serving platter. Garnish with fresh herbs and serve with lemon slices.

★

SWEET AND SOUR SHRIMP

This dish will not be as red as traditionally prepared restaurant fare because of the omission of red food coloring.

YIELD: 6–8 SERVINGS

3 pounds large or jumbo shrimp
⅓ cup dry sherry
1 teaspoon tamari soy sauce
1 teaspoon ground ginger
6 dried shitaki mushrooms
2 cups hot water
1 tablespoon sherry
2 cups cornstarch
2 medium carrots
2 medium bell peppers (about 1 cup chopped)
2 medium yellow onions
6 ounces canned bamboo shoots

3 large green onions
8 cloves garlic
¼ cup julienne of peeled fresh ginger
2 cups cubed fresh pineapple
oil for frying the shrimp
1 teaspoon sesame oil
¾ cup honey
½ cup raspberry vinegar
1½ cups stock or water
1 tablespoon cornstarch
2 teaspoons tamari soy sauce
¼ teaspoon cayenne pepper

1 Devein and peel shrimp, removing tails (see *Shrimp*).

2 Marinate shrimp in a mixing bowl 15 to 30 minutes with sherry, tamari soy sauce, and ground ginger. Stir shrimp around to cover evenly with marinade.

3 While shrimp are marinating, soak

dried shitaki mushrooms in hot water combined with 1 tablespoon sherry 15 to 30 minutes.

4 Place cornstarch in a long, shallow dish. Dredge shrimp in cornstarch, making sure each is well coated. Lay coated shrimp on waxed-paper-covered baking sheet and refrigerate until ready to cook.

5 Slice carrots on the bias, no wider than about ⅛ inch.

6 Cut bell peppers into 1½-inch cubes.

7 Coarsely chop yellow onions.

8 Drain canned bamboo shoots and cut into thin julienne strips.

9 Split green onions and cut into 1½-inch sections.

10 Peel garlic and slice thinly.

11 Peel ginger and cut into julienne strips.

12 Peel and core fresh pineapple and cut into ½-inch cubes.

13 Drain mushrooms, remove stems, blot out moisture on paper towels, and slice thinly.

14 Combine carrots, bell peppers, onions, bamboo shoots, green onions, garlic, pineapple, and mushrooms and set aside.

15 In a large skillet, heat enough oil to cover 1 layer of shrimp. Remove shrimp from refrigerator and cook 1 layer of shrimp in the pan at a time. Turn 1 or 2 times until shrimp turns golden. Drain on paper towels and repeat until all shrimp is cooked. Reserve cooked shrimp in a warm place.

16 Pour off all but 2 or 3 tablespoons of oil from skillet. Add sesame oil to skillet and return to high heat.

17 Add reserved vegetables and pineapple chunks to skillet all at once, and stir constantly 6 or 7 minutes. Do not overcook; vegetables should be crisp.

18 Combine honey, raspberry vinegar, and 1 cup of the stock or water. Blend and add to cooking vegetables. Reduce heat to simmer.

19 Blend 1 tablespoon cornstarch, 2 teaspoons tamari soy sauce, and cayenne pepper with remaining ½ cup stock or water. Add to simmering mixture in skillet and stir while dish thickens.

20 Add cooked shrimp to skillet and stir to coat shrimp thoroughly with sauce.

21 Remove from heat and serve as quickly as possible.

★

REDI-MIX SAUTÉED REDFISH WITH CRABMEAT

YIELD: 4-6 SERVINGS

2 pounds boned fillet of redfish
juice of 3 lemons
1 cup unbleached white flour
1 teaspoon ground black pepper
1 cup milk
1 tablespoon paprika

1 cup Redi-Mix (page 128)
1 teaspoon garlic powder
1 cup oil
¼ cup unsalted margarine or butter
1 pint lump crabmeat (approximately 10 ounces)

2 tablespoons crème fraîche or sour
cream

Tabasco sauce to taste
4 green onions or scallions, chopped

1 Cut redfish into serving pieces (approximately 4 ounces each) and
sprinkle with juice of 1 lemon.
2 Combine flour and black pepper in
a shallow dish. Combine milk and
paprika in a bowl. Combine Redi-
Mix and garlic powder in another
shallow dish.
3 Dredge redfish fillets in flour, dip
into milk, then coat with Redi-Mix.
4 Heat oil in large skillet.
5 Add breaded fillets and reduce heat
to medium, gently cooking each
side until the fish is a nice golden
brown color. If heat is too high,
crust will be overcooked and fish
will be undercooked.

6 Drain fillets on paper towels and
arrange on a warm serving platter.
7 Melt margarine or butter in a
skillet or sauté pan.
8 Add crabmeat, crème fraîche or
sour cream, juice of remaining 2
lemons, and generous amount of
Tabasco sauce.
9 Stir gently to blend. Be careful not
to break up the lumps of crabmeat.
10 Heat only until mixture is hot.
11 Turn burner off. Stir in chopped
green onions or scallions, and
spoon mixture over fillets. Serve
immediately.

★

POACHED FISH ROLLS

YIELD: 4 SERVINGS

2 pounds boned fillet of sole
juice of 1 lemon
4 teaspoons paprika
½ teaspoon cayenne pepper
3 cups dry white wine
2 cups Court Bouillon (page 39)
   or water

8 white peppercorns
8 black peppercorns
6 whole cloves
3 dashes of bitters
1 tablespoon chopped parsley
1 clove garlic

1 Cut each fillet of sole into strips
about 2 inches wide and 8 inches
long. Make sure all bones are
removed.
2 Lay strips of sole together on work
surface and sprinkle on one side
with lemon juice, paprika, and cayenne pepper.
3 Starting with the small end, roll
strips of sole into tight rounds, seasoned side inward. Secure with

wooden toothpick. Set rolled fish in
refrigerator until ready to poach.
4 In a fish poacher or a large skillet
(not aluminum or cast-iron), combine white wine, court bouillon or
water, white and black peppercorns, cloves, and bitters. Bring liquid to boil and reduce to simmer.
5 Allow poaching liquid to simmer
about 10 minutes, then add rolled
fillets of sole. Cover and poach 4 to

5 minutes, depending on size of fillets. Do not overcook.

6 While fish is poaching, chop together parsley and garlic. Moisten with 1 teaspoon hot poaching liquid.

7 Remove poached fillets from liquid and arrange on a warm serving platter or plates. Carefully remove toothpicks. Sprinkle with parsley-garlic topping and serve immediately.

★

GRILLED FRESH CATFISH

This fish makes such a delicate, savory dish that no sauce is needed.

YIELD: 6 SERVINGS

¼ cup safflower oil
2 tablespoons tamari soy sauce
1 teaspoon ground ginger

½ teaspoon white pepper
6 steaks of fresh catfish, 1 inch thick

1 Combine safflower oil, tamari soy sauce, ginger, and white pepper and brush onto steaks.

2 Allow to stand 15 minutes.
3 Grill (see *Grilling*) approximately 2 to 3 minutes per side.

★

FENNEL-SMOKED FISH

Donald Wertz

———

Smoking fish is tricky business. Shellfish, particularly, tend to turn mushy. Fillets of delicate whitefish, such as flounder or sole, are very difficult to turn without crumbling them. It is advisable to cover the smoker rack with ¼-inch-mesh hardware cloth, which will give more support for the fish, and to begin by grilling salmon or swordfish steaks or whole fish such as trout, which hold together better and are more easily turned.

fish (whole, steaks, or fillets) in desired quantity
2 handfuls fennel stalks
2 quarts water

¼ cup lemon juice
1⅓ cup chopped parsley
white pepper

1 Soak fennel stalks in water to cover for 30 minutes.
2 Bring mixture of 2 quarts water, lemon juice, and parsley to a boil. Keep hot.

3 Wash and dry fish; place on mesh-covered smoker rack.
4 Sprinkle with white pepper.
5 Drain fennel stalks; toss onto hot coals.

6 Set smoker pan into smoker and carefully pour flavored water into pan.

7 Set prepared fish into smoker and close lid. Steaks and fillets should be cooked 8 to 12 minutes on each side, depending on thickness and size. Whitefish will take 10 to 15 minutes a side.

Variation

In step 2, instead of water, lemon juice, and parsley, use 2 quarts dry white wine and 1⅓ cup chopped parsley.

9

BREADS

YEAST BREADS

★

WHOLE WHEAT BREAD

Dianne Ezernack and I developed this good basic recipe at the Baker's Family Bake Shop in Knoxville, Tennessee. It lends itself well to many variations.

YIELD: 3 MEDIUM LOAVES

2 tablespoons active dry yeast
2 tablespoons oil
¼ cup honey or sugar (honey will make a richer, moister bread that will stay fresh longer)
2 cups warm water

2 teaspoons salt (optional)
2 cups unbleached white flour
4 cups whole wheat flour (approximate)
1 egg, beaten
1 tablespoon sesame or poppy seeds

1 In a large bowl combine yeast, oil, and honey or sugar. Thoroughly mix in warm water. Allow yeast to activate for 10 minutes in a warm area.

2 When yeast has foamed, add salt if desired, unbleached white flour, and whole wheat flour (figure 13a).

3 Knead on floured surface until elastic and smooth (figure 13b). Oil dough, replace in bowl, and cover with damp cloth. Allow to rise 1 hour, or until doubled in bulk (figure 13c).

4 Beat dough down and allow to rise 30 minutes more.

5 Knead again, form into loaves, and place in greased bread pans (figure 13d). Let rise until doubled in bulk.

6 Carefully brush with beaten egg, sprinkle with sesame or poppy seeds, and bake in 350° oven 30 to 45 minutes, depending on size of loaves.

★

FRENCH BREAD STICKS

YIELD: 32 BREAD STICKS

2 tablespoons active dry yeast
2 tablespoons honey or raw turbinado sugar
2 tablespoons olive oil
2 cups warm water

1 tablespoon salt
6–8 cups unbleached white flour
1 egg white
5 tablespoons sesame or poppy seeds

Figure 13a

Figure 13b

Figure 13c

Figure 13d

1 In a large bowl, mix yeast, honey or
   sugar, and olive oil. Add warm water
   and mix thoroughly. Allow yeast to
   activate for 10 minutes in a warm
   area.

2 When yeast has foamed, add salt
   and mix in unbleached white flour
   until dough is very stiff.

3 Knead until dough is elastic and
   smooth. Oil dough, replace in bowl,

and cover with a damp cloth. Allow
to rise 1 hour.

4 Oil a baking sheet and sprinkle with
   cornmeal.

5 After dough has risen, beat it down
   and knead slightly. Divide into 32
   equal pieces by cutting the dough
   in half, quarters, and so forth.

6 Roll each piece into a rope 8 or 10
   inches long (figure 14a). Place on

baking sheet and brush lightly with water (figure 14b). Allow to rise until doubled in bulk, 30 to 45 minutes.

7 Brush bread sticks lightly with water again.

8 Bake in preheated 350° oven until slightly brown.

9 Remove from oven and brush with egg white, then sprinkle with sesame or poppy seeds. Return to oven for 5 to 10 minutes, or until bread sticks are a rich golden color.

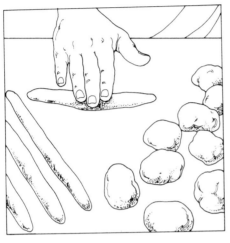

Figure 14a

Figure 14b

★

OATMEAL-HONEY BREAD

Betty Wertz

YIELD: 2 LOAVES

1½ cups boiling water
1 cup oatmeal
½ cup honey
⅓ cup vegetable shortening
1 tablespoon salt

2 eggs
2 cups whole wheat flour
2 packages active dry yeast
½ cup warm water
4 cups all-purpose flour

1 Preheat oven to 350°.

2 Mix boiling water, oatmeal, honey, shortening, and salt in large bowl. Cool to lukewarm.

3 Beat eggs.

4 Stir whole wheat flour and eggs into oatmeal mixture.

5 Dissolve yeast in warm water and beat into the mixture.

6 Beat in all-purpose flour, 2 cups at a time.

7 On floured board, knead dough about 10 minutes, until smooth.

8 Shape into 2 loaves. Let rise until doubled in bulk.

9 Bake at 350° about 25 minutes.

★

CHALLAH BREAD

Inspired by a recipe by Kelly McCormick.

YIELD: 2 LOAVES

*4 or more cups unbleached white
   flour*
2 tablespoons sugar
1 teaspoon salt
2 tablespoons active dry yeast
*5 tablespoons unsalted margarine
   or butter*

1 cup very warm water
few strands of saffron
4 eggs
1 beaten egg

1 Sift together 2 cups flour, sugar, salt, and yeast. Place in a large bowl and set aside.

2 Melt margarine or butter.

3 Mix melted margarine or butter and warm water. Mix in saffron and gradually add to sifted dry ingredients.

4 Beat 2 minutes and set aside for another couple of minutes.

5 Add 4 eggs one at a time, beating a bit after each addition.

6 Stir in 1 cup flour and continue mixing for 2 minutes.

7 Gradually add remaining flour until mixture forms a dough.

8 On a floured surface, knead the dough until it is smooth and elastic, but not sticky.

9 Lightly oil dough and place in a large oiled bowl. Cover with a damp towel and allow to rise in a warm place about 1 hour.

10 Punch down dough and divide in half (with hands, not a knife). Then divide each half into 3 equal pieces.

11 On a floured surface, roll each piece of dough into a thin foot-long rope.

12 Braid 3 ropes together, seal ends with water, and repeat with other 3 ropes.

13 Place loaves on baking sheets sprinkled with cornmeal and allow to rise 30 minutes.

14 While bread is rising, preheat oven to 350°.

15 Bake risen loaves 20 minutes.

16 Remove from oven. Brush with beaten egg and bake 10 or 15 minutes longer.

★

MIRACLE BREAD

This is a heavy, nutritious, good-tasting bread featuring complementary proteins.

YIELD: 3 LOAVES

3 cups potato water (the cooking water left from boiling or steaming potatoes)
3 tablespoons active dry yeast
2 tablespoons blackstrap molasses
½ cup honey
¼ cup extra virgin olive oil
2 cups unbleached white flour
3 tablespoons millet
½ cup rolled oats

½ teaspoon salt
1 cup rye flour
1 cup buckwheat flour
1 cup soy flour
½ cup wheat bran
¼ cup cornmeal
½ cup barley flour
3 cups whole wheat flour
1–2 tablespoons cooking oil
1 egg, beaten

1 Heat potato water to warm and combine in a large mixing bowl with yeast, molasses, honey, and olive oil.

2 Set mixing bowl in a warm place and allow yeast to activate for 12 minutes.

3 Stir in unbleached white flour, millet, and rolled oats. Blend well and allow to rise 5 to 10 minutes.

4 Stir in salt, rye flour, buckwheat flour, soy flour, wheat bran, cornmeal, barley flour, and whole wheat flour. Blend well after each addition.

5 Knead until dough is elastic and smooth. Oil dough with cooking oil, replace in bowl, and cover with a damp cloth. Allow to rise in a warm place 1 hour and 15 minutes.

6 Beat dough down and knead slightly. Divide into 3 equal pieces and form loaves.

7 Place loaves into greased bread pans and allow to rise 45 minutes. Preheat oven to 350°.

8 Bake risen loaves 30 minutes. Remove from oven, brush with beaten egg, and bake another 10 to 15 minutes.

★

NANNIE'S ROLLS

YIELD: 2 DOZEN LARGE DINNER ROLLS

2 tablespoons active dry yeast
2 tablespoons cooking oil
½ cup honey
2 cups warm water

1 teaspoon salt (optional)
5–6 cups unbleached white flour or a combination of whole wheat and unbleached white

1 Preheat oven to 350°.
2 Mix yeast, oil, honey, and warm water and allow yeast to activate in a warm place for 10 minutes.
3 Add salt if desired. Stir in flour until dough is too thick to stir.
4 Add rest of flour a little at a time and knead by hand until dough is smooth and elastic.
5 Oil dough, place in an oiled bowl, and cover with a warm, damp towel. Allow to rise in a warm place for about an hour.
6 When dough has doubled in bulk, punch down and allow to rise 20 more minutes.
7 Turn onto a floured surface and knead for a few minutes more, then divide into 24 equal pieces.
8 For soft rolls, dip shaped rolls into melted margarine or butter and place them side by side in a large baking dish. For chewier rolls, omit dipping into butter and place in greased muffin tins.
9 Allow to rise until doubled in bulk.
10 Bake at 350° for 35 to 40 minutes or until golden brown.

★

GRAHAM ROLLS

Nita Graves

YIELD: 2–3 DOZEN DINNER ROLLS

2 tablespoons active dry yeast
1 cup warm water
1 cup bran cereal
½ cup raw turbinado sugar
½ teaspoon salt
¾ cup unsalted margarine or butter, softened

1 cup boiling water
2 eggs, slightly beaten
2½ cups unbleached white flour (approximate)
2½ cups whole wheat flour (approximate)

1 Dissolve yeast in warm water. Mix together and stir until cool.
2 In a large bread bowl, combine bran cereal, sugar, salt, margarine or butter, and boiling water. Stir until blended.
3 Add yeast and beaten eggs.
4 Stir in unbleached white flour and whole wheat flour. Mix until elastic and smooth.
5 Oil top of dough, cover with a damp cloth, and place in refrigerator for 24 hours.
6 Remove dough from refrigerator and knead on a floured surface 3 to 5 minutes.
7 Shape into individual rolls and place in oiled baking dishes.
8 Let rolls rise another 45 minutes to 1 hour in a warm place.
9 Bake in preheated 400° oven for about 15 minutes.

QUICK BREADS

★

PUMPKIN BREAD
YIELD: 3 MEDIUM LOAVES

2 cups fresh pureed pumpkin or
canned pumpkin (1-pound can)
3½ cups sifted unbleached white
flour
1 teaspoon low-sodium baking
powder or ½ teaspoon regular
baking powder
2 teaspoons baking soda

1 teaspoon nutmeg
1 teaspoon ground cloves
1 teaspoon cinnamon
4 eggs
3 cups raw turbinado sugar
⅔ cup water
1 cup unsalted margarine or butter

1 Preheat oven to 350°.
2 Prepare fresh pumpkin (see *Pumpkin*) and set aside 2 cups puree.
3 Sift together flour, baking powder, baking soda, nutmeg, cloves, and cinnamon and set aside.
4 Beat eggs, add sugar, and beat until creamy.

5 Add pureed pumpkin, water, and margarine or butter. Blend thoroughly.
6 Add sifted dry ingredients and mix until completely blended.
7 Grease 3 loaf pans and pour a third of the batter into each pan.
8 Bake approximately 1 hour at 350°.

★

BRAN MUFFINS
YIELD: 12 MUFFINS

1¼ cups unbleached white flour
2 tablespoons low-sodium baking
powder or 1 tablespoon regular
baking powder
½ cup raw turbinado sugar

1½ cups bran cereal
1¼ cups yogurt
1 egg
⅓ cup vegetable oil

1 Preheat oven to 400°.
2 Stir together flour, baking powder, and sugar. Set aside.
3 Combine bran cereal and yogurt in a mixing bowl. Let stand 1 or 2 minutes or until cereal is softened.

4 Add egg and vegetable oil and beat well by hand.
5 Add dry ingredients to cereal mixture, stirring only until combined.
6 Divide batter evenly into 12 greased 2½-inch muffin cups.

7 Bake at 400° about 25 minutes or until muffins are golden brown.

Serve warm or allow to cool and store in airtight container.

★

OAT BRAN MUFFINS

Rachel Cohen and Kathryn Counts

YIELD: 16–18 MUFFINS

2½ cups oat bran
3 tablespoons low-sodium baking powder or 4½ teaspoons regular baking powder
½ cup raisins or blueberries

2 eggs
1 cup milk
½ cup maple syrup or ⅓ cup maple syrup and 1 mashed banana

1 Preheat oven to 400°. Grease muffin tins or line with paper baking cups.
2 In a mixing bowl, combine oat bran, baking powder, and raisins or blueberries.
3 In a separate bowl, combine eggs, milk, maple syrup, and banana.

4 Add the wet ingredients to the dry, mix lightly, and immediately put in muffin tins.
5 Place in oven, reduce heat to 375°, and bake 15 to 20 minutes until lightly browned.

★

CHEDDAR CHEESE MUFFINS

A favorite in cooking classes for children.

YIELD: 12 MUFFINS

¾ cup grated cheddar cheese
5 tablespoons unsalted margarine or butter
¾ cup whole wheat flour
¾ cup wheat germ
5 teaspoons low-sodium baking powder or 2½ teaspoons regular baking powder

½ teaspoon salt
1 egg
3 tablespoons honey
½ cup low-fat yogurt or sour milk (see Sour Milk)

1 Preheat oven to 425°.
2 Grate cheddar cheese and mix with 2 tablespoons softened margarine or butter.
3 In a mixing bowl, combine whole

wheat flour, wheat germ, baking powder, and salt. Mix well and make a depression in the middle.
4 Melt remaining 3 tablespoons margarine or butter, beat egg, and com-

bine both with yogurt or sour milk and honey. Pour into depression in wheat mixture and stir only until mixed. The batter should be lumpy.

5 Pour batter into greased muffin tins and press a little of the cheese and butter mixture into each muffin.
6 Bake at 425° about 25 minutes.

★

WHOLE WHEAT SCONES

Muriel Nelson

YIELD: 12 SCONES

2 cups whole wheat flour
2 tablespoons low-sodium baking powder or 1 tablespoon regular baking powder

3 tablespoons oil or unsalted butter
1 egg, slightly beaten
½ cup milk or yogurt

1 Preheat oven to 400°.
2 In a large mixing bowl, sift together flour and baking powder.
3 Add oil or small pieces of butter, and crumb mixture with a fork or a pastry blender.
4 Stir in beaten egg and milk or yogurt.
5 Stir until mixture forms a dough,

and shape into a flattened round (approximately ¾ inch thick) on a lightly floured surface. Cut into 12 wedges.
6 Lay pieces on an oiled baking sheet and bake at 400° about 15 minutes, or until scones are done to the touch.

★

WESTLAKE SCONES NO. 1

YIELD: 12 SCONES

¼ cup Irish oatmeal
¾ cup low-fat yogurt
1½ cups whole wheat pastry flour
1½ cups unbleached white flour
¾ cup raw turbinado sugar
3 tablespoons low-sodium baking powder or 4½ teaspoons regular baking powder

¼ cup unsalted margarine or butter
¾ cup chopped walnuts
1 egg
1 tablespoon almond extract
1 tablespoon vanilla extract

1 Preheat oven to 350°.
2 Mix Irish oatmeal and yogurt and set aside for 15 minutes.
3 In a large mixing bowl, sift together

whole wheat pastry flour, unbleached white flour, and baking powder.
4 Add sugar.

5 Add margarine or butter, cut into small bits, and crumb mixture with fork or pastry blender.
6 Stir in chopped walnuts.
7 Mix in egg, oatmeal-yogurt mixture, and almond and vanilla extracts.
8 Stir until mixture forms a dough, and shape into a flattened round (approximately ¾ inch thick) on a lightly floured surface.
9 Sprinkle top of dough with un-bleached white flour, and cut into 12 wedges.
10 Lay wedges on an oiled baking sheet and bake at 350° about 20 minutes, or until scones are lightly browned.

★

WESTLAKE SCONES NO. 2

YIELD: 12 SCONES

¼ cup Irish oatmeal
¾ cup low-fat yogurt
1½ cups whole wheat pastry flour
1½ cups unbleached white flour
3 tablespoons low-sodium baking powder or 4½ teaspoons regular baking powder
¾ cup raw turbinado sugar
¼ cup oat bran
¼ cup wheat bran
¼ cup unsalted margarine or butter
1 egg, slightly beaten
1 tablespoon vanilla extract

1 Preheat oven to 350°.
2 Mix Irish oatmeal and yogurt and set aside for 15 minutes.
3 In a large mixing bowl, sift together whole wheat pastry flour, un-bleached white flour, and baking powder.
4 Add oat bran, wheat bran, and sugar.
5 Add margarine or butter, cut into small bits, and crumb mixture with a fork or a pastry blender.
6 Mix in egg, oatmeal-yogurt mixture, and vanilla extract.
7 Stir until mixture forms a dough, and shape into a flattened round (approximately ¾ inch thick) on a lightly floured surface.
8 Sprinkle top of dough with un-bleached white flour and cut into 12 wedges.
9 Lay wedges on an oiled baking sheet and bake at 350° about 15 minutes, or until scones are lightly browned.

★

GARLIC TOAST

YIELD: 1 LOAF

4 cloves garlic
½ cup unsalted margarine or butter
1 loaf French bread

1 Finely chop garlic.
2 Lightly sauté garlic in margarine or butter.
3 Split French bread lengthwise.

4 Spread garlic and margarine mixture on bread.
5 Lightly toast bread. Serve with pasta and Creole dishes.

★

SALAD CROUTONS WITH HERBS

YIELD: ABOUT 2 QUARTS

1 loaf Whole Wheat Bread (page 175) or commercial whole wheat bread
1 stick unsalted margarine or butter

1 tablespoon minced garlic or garlic powder
1 tablespoon thyme
1 tablespoon dill weed

1 Preheat oven to 400°.
2 Cut bread into small cubes.
3 Line a baking sheet with foil and spread bread cubes evenly about.
4 Place baking sheet in oven for 5 minutes.
5 While bread cubes are toasting, melt margarine or butter and add garlic or garlic powder, thyme, and dill weed.

6 Remove bread cubes from oven and pour herb mixture on them. Toss lightly and return to oven. Bake about 10 more minutes, tossing occasionally.
7 Remove from oven when croutons are dark brown and allow to cool. Store in airtight container at room temperature. Croutons will stay fresh several weeks.

★

DOWN-HOME HUSH PUPPIES

Traditionally served with fried fish.

YIELD: ABOUT 4 DOZEN PIECES

1¾ cups white cornmeal
¼ cup unbleached white flour
4 teaspoons low-sodium baking

powder or 2 teaspoons regular baking powder
¼ teaspoon salt

1 teaspoon raw turbinado sugar
1 egg
2 cups low-fat milk or water

*½ cup chopped green onions
  (3 or 4)*
enough oil to deep-fry

1 In a mixing bowl, combine cornmeal, flour, baking powder, salt, and
sugar.

2 In another bowl, beat together egg,
milk or water, and chopped green
onions.

3 Stir wet ingredients into dry and
mix until smooth.

4 Heat oil in large frying pan and
when hot, drop batter into hot oil
by large tablespoonfuls. Cook to a
nice golden color.

5 Drain and serve hot.

★

WHOLE WHEAT PANCAKES OR WAFFLES

Betty Wertz

———

The best whole wheat pancakes we've ever had; a never-fail recipe.

YIELD: 8–10 PANCAKES

1 egg
1 cup buttermilk
2 tablespoons cooking oil
¾ cup whole wheat flour
1 tablespoon honey
2 teaspoons low-sodium baking

powder or *1 teaspoon regular
  baking powder*
½ teaspoon baking soda
*¼ cup coarsely chopped pecans
  (optional)*

1 Beat egg slightly, then add rest of
ingredients.

2 Beat only until blended, leaving
batter a little bit lumpy.

3 Cook on hot griddle, turning once,
as with any other pancake.

10

DESSERTS

C O O K I E S

★

R E F R I G E R A T O R   C O O K I E S

Inspired by a recipe by Barbara Wade, this is a wonderful basic cookie recipe that lends itself to many variations. Try adding extracts, cocoa, chocolate or butterscotch chips, nuts, fruit, or whatever your imagination suggests.

Y I E L D :   A B O U T   4   D O Z E N   C O O K I E S

½ cup unsalted margarine or butter, softened
1 cup fructose
1 egg
1 teaspoon vanilla extract

1½ cups unbleached white flour
½ teaspoon baking soda
⅛ teaspoon salt
1 cup nuts, raisins, chocolate chips, etc. (optional)

1 Preheat oven to 375°.
2 Cream margarine or butter, fructose, egg, and vanilla extract.
3 Sift together flour, baking soda, and salt.
4 Add sifted dry ingredients to the creamed mixture and beat until smooth.

5 Stir in nuts, raisins, or chocolate chips if desired.
6 Roll into a long, round roll and cover with plastic wrap.
7 Place in freezer at least 12 hours.
8 Cut into ¼-inch slices and bake 12 minutes in preheated 375° oven on greased and floured cookie sheets.

★

G R A N D M O T H E R' S   S U G A R   C O O K I E S   N O.   1

Traditionally made by hand because the dough is so thick.

Y I E L D :   4 – 5   D O Z E N   C O O K I E S

3 cups unbleached white flour
2 teaspoons low-sodium baking powder or 1 teaspoon regular baking powder

1 cup unsalted margarine or butter
1½ cups raw turbinado sugar
3 eggs
1 teaspoon vanilla extract

1 Preheat oven to 375°.
2 Sift together flour and baking powder and set aside.

3 Using a wooden spoon, cream together margarine or butter and sugar in a mixing bowl.

4 Slightly beat eggs and vanilla extract and add to creamed mixture. Blend thoroughly.

5 Add sifted flour and baking powder and mix into dough.

6 Grease and flour baking sheets.

7 Roll out cookie dough on well-floured surface to about ¼ inch thick.

8 Cut out cookies with any kind of cookie cutter. Arrange cookies on baking sheet and sprinkle with sugar or leave plain. Cookies can also be decorated with nuts, dried fruits, or candies.

9 Bake 10 minutes at 375°. Cookies will be light golden.

10 After baking, remove from pan with spatula, cool, and store in an airtight container.

★

GRANDMOTHER'S SUGAR COOKIES NO. 2

YIELD: ABOUT 4 DOZEN COOKIES

3 cups unbleached white flour
1 teaspoon low-sodium baking powder or ½ teaspoon regular baking powder
½ teaspoon baking soda

1 cup unsalted margarine or butter (room temperature)
2 eggs
1 cup sugar
1 teaspoon vanilla extract

1 Preheat oven to 375°.

2 Sift dry ingredients into mixing bowl and blend in margarine or butter until mixture resembles cornmeal.

3 In a separate bowl beat eggs, then add sugar and vanilla extract and mix well.

4 Blend egg and sugar mixture into flour mixture to form dough.

5 Chill dough at least 2 hours.

6 Roll out cold dough on floured surface and cut into desired shapes.

7 Bake on greased and floured baking sheet 5 to 8 minutes at 375°.

★

GRANDMOTHER'S GINGERSNAPS

YIELD: 4 DOZEN COOKIES OR MORE

½ cup unsalted margarine or butter
1 cup fructose
4 cups sifted unbleached white flour
½ teaspoon baking soda

1 tablespoon ground ginger
½ cup water
½ cup molasses

1 Preheat oven to 400°.

2 With an electric mixer, cream margarine or butter and gradually add fructose.

3 Sift flour before measuring, and mix with baking soda and ground ginger.

4 Add flour to creamed mixture alternately with water and molasses.

5 Roll out dough onto floured surface until very thin. Cut out cookies with a small round cutter.

6 Grease and flour baking sheets, lay cookies on pan, and brush cookies with water.

7 Bake 7 minutes and quickly remove from pan with a spatula.

★

FAMILY HEIRLOOM TEA CAKES

My updated version of an old-fashioned cookie recipe handed down in my family from the nineteenth century.

YIELD: 5 DOZEN COOKIES

1½ cups raw turbinado sugar
1 cup unsalted margarine or butter
3 eggs
1 teaspoon vanilla extract
1 teaspoon baking soda

1 tablespoon water
2 teaspoons cream of tartar
3½ cups unbleached white flour
½ teaspoon salt (optional)

1 Preheat oven to 350°.

2 Cream together sugar and margarine or butter.

3 Blend in eggs and vanilla extract.

4 Dissolve baking soda in water and add to creamed sugar and margarine or butter.

5 Add cream of tartar.

6 Blend in flour, about 1 cup at a time. Also add salt at this time, if desired.

7 Mix well and drop by teaspoonfuls on greased cookie sheet. Bake at 350° for 5 or 6 minutes. Cookies are done when they are very lightly browned on the bottom.

★

HONEY BALLS

Betty Wertz

YIELD: 6 DOZEN COOKIES

1 cup unsalted margarine or butter
½ cup honey
2 cups flour

½ teaspoon salt
2 teaspoons vanilla extract
2 cups chopped pecans

1 Cream margarine or butter.
2 Add honey, flour, salt, and vanilla extract and mix well.
3 Stir in chopped pecans. Chill 2 hours.

4 Preheat oven to 325°.
5 Roll dough into small balls and bake on greased cookie sheet at 325° for 20 minutes.

★

PEANUT BUTTER TREATS

Jim Carter

An unbaked natural-food confection.

YIELD: 9–10 DOZEN PIECES

4 cups crunchy peanut butter
1 cup tahini (sesame butter)
½ cup honey
½ cup molasses

1¾ cups raw wheat germ
2 cups chopped nuts
1½–2 cups coconut

1 Mix thoroughly all ingredients except coconut. Cover and chill, overnight if possible.
2 Spread coconut on a baking sheet and bake at 400°, stirring often, about 5 minutes or until coconut turns golden.

3 Remove dough from refrigerator and shape into small round balls (about 1 inch in diameter).
4 Roll candy balls in toasted coconut and reserve on waxed-paper-lined trays. Serve chilled.

CAKES

★

BANANA-HONEY CUPCAKES

YIELD: 24 CUPCAKES

4 ripe bananas
1¼ cups unbleached white flour
1 cup whole wheat flour
1 tablespoon baking soda
½ teaspoon salt
½ cup unsalted margarine or butter

¾ cup honey
2 eggs
1 tablespoon vanilla extract
½ teaspoon almond extract
1 tablespoon cinnamon
¾ cup chopped nuts (optional)

1 Preheat oven to 375°.
2 Mash bananas with a fork.
3 Sift together unbleached white flour, whole wheat flour, baking soda, and salt.
4 Combine margarine or butter, honey, and eggs and mix until smooth.

5 Add vanilla extract, almond extract, and cinnamon.
6 Mix in ripe bananas.
7 Combine flour mixture and banana mixture, and stir in nuts if desired.
8 Pour into greased and floured cupcake tins and bake in 375° oven about 20 to 25 minutes.

★

CRANBERRY UPSIDE-DOWN CAKE

This delightful little cake is our version of a recipe from Gourmet *magazine, November 1980.*

YIELD: ONE 9-INCH CAKE

1 pound fresh cranberries
9 tablespoons unsalted margarine or butter, softened
1 cup fructose
1 large egg
1 teaspoon vanilla extract
1 teaspoon minced orange rind

1¼ cups unbleached white flour
1 tablespoon low-sodium baking powder or 1½ teaspoons regular baking powder
½ cup sour milk (see Sour Milk*)*
⅓ cup red currant jelly
whipped cream

1 Preheat oven to 350°.
2 Rinse cranberries, pick over, and pat dry.

3 With 3 tablespoons margarine or butter, grease bottom and sides of a 9-inch round cake pan (1¼ inches

deep). Sprinkle ½ cup fructose evenly over bottom, and arrange cranberries in pan.

4 In a bowl, cream together 6 table-spoons margarine or butter and ½ cup fructose. Add egg, vanilla extract, and orange rind, and beat until well combined.

5 In another bowl, sift together flour and baking powder. Stir flour mixture into margarine mixture, ½ cup at a time, alternately with sour milk. Stir just until combined.

6 Pour batter over cranberries, smooth top, and bake on a baking sheet in the middle of a preheated 350° oven 1 hour, or until browned.

7 Transfer cake to a rack and let cool in the pan 20 minutes. Run a thin knife around inside of pan and invert cake onto a cake stand.

8 In a small saucepan, heat red currant jelly over low heat, stirring until melted. Brush melted jelly over the cake. Serve warm with sweetened whipped cream.

★

SCOTTISH OATMEAL CAKE

YIELD: 1 LARGE TUBE CAKE

1 cup oatmeal
1 cup cream
½ cup unsalted margarine or butter
1 cup brown or raw turbinado sugar
1 egg
1 teaspoon baking soda
2 teaspoons low-sodium baking powder or *1 teaspoon regular baking powder*
1 teaspoon cinnamon

1 teaspoon ground ginger
1 teaspoon ground cloves
1 teaspoon vanilla extract
2 cups unbleached white flour

Topping
2 tablespoons flour
2 tablespoons unsalted margarine or butter
5 tablespoons sugar

1 Preheat oven to 350°.
2 Soak oatmeal in cream and set aside.
3 Cream margarine or butter and sugar, add egg, and mix well.
4 Sift dry ingredients and add to margarine mixture a little at a time, alternating with oatmeal mixture. Mix until batter is thick and smooth.

5 Turn into greased and floured tube cake pan.
6 Blend topping ingredients together with fingers, and sprinkle evenly on top of cake. Pat smooth and bake 1 hour in preheated 350° oven.

★

OL'-TIMEY RUM CAKE

A dessert that demands dark, rich coffee.

YIELD: 1 LARGE TUBE CAKE

½ cup shortening
½ cup unsalted margarine or butter
2 cups sugar
4 eggs
1 teaspoon vanilla extract
1 teaspoon lemon extract
1 teaspoon rum extract
3 cups unbleached white flour
½ teaspoon baking soda

1 teaspoon low-sodium baking
   powder or ½ teaspoon regular
   baking powder
1 cup buttermilk

Topping
1 cup sugar
½ cup water
2 teaspoons rum extract

1 Preheat oven to 350°.
2 Oil a tube or fluted tube pan and
   dust with flour.
3 For 2½ minutes beat the following
   ingredients in an electric mixer:
   shortening, margarine or butter,
   sugar, eggs, and lemon, vanilla, and
   rum extracts.
4 Sift together flour, soda, and baking
   powder and add alternately with

   buttermilk to ingredients in mixer.
5 Bake at 350° about 65 minutes.
6 While cake is baking, combine topping ingredients and bring to a rolling boil. Set aside and cool to room
   temperature.
7 Remove cake from oven. Pour
   cooled topping on hot cake and allow cake to cool in pan. Remove
   from pan when cool.

★

NORTH TEXAS LEMON POUND CAKE

YIELD: 1 LARGE TUBE OR LOAF CAKE

3 cups sifted unbleached white flour
½ teaspoon baking soda
1 teaspoon low-sodium baking
   powder or ½ teaspoon regular
   baking powder
2 cups fructose
4 eggs

1 cup unsalted margarine or butter
1½ teaspoons lemon extract
peel of 1 lemon, grated and finely
   chopped
1 teaspoon vanilla extract
1 cup buttermilk or yogurt

1 Heat oven to 350°.
2 Grease large tube or loaf pan and
   dust with flour.

3 Sift together dry ingredients in mixing bowl.

4 In a mixer combine eggs, margarine or butter, lemon extract, lemon peel, and vanilla extract.

5 Add dry ingredients alternately with buttermilk or yogurt to mixing bowl. Beat until smooth.

6 Pour into tube or loaf pan. Bake 1 hour and 10 minutes at 350° until done.

7 Let cool 10 minutes. Remove from pan and wrap in foil. Will keep a week or more.

★

GINGERBREAD

YIELD: 12 LARGE PIECES

½ cup unsalted margarine or butter
½ cup raw turbinado sugar
1 cup molasses
2 eggs
1 teaspoon vanilla extract
2 cups sifted unbleached white flour

1 teaspoon baking soda
2 teaspoons ground ginger
½ teaspoon cinnamon
¼ teaspoon ground cardamom
½ cup low-fat milk

1 Preheat oven to 350°. Grease a 9-by-12-inch baking pan and line it with waxed paper.

2 With an electric mixer, cream margarine or butter and gradually add sugar.

3 Add molasses, eggs, and vanilla extract and beat thoroughly.

4 Mix sifted flour (sift before measuring) with baking soda, ground ginger, cinnamon, and ground cardamom.

5 Add flour mixture alternately with milk to mixing bowl. Beat well after each addition.

6 Pour into prepared pan and bake at 350° for 45 minutes. Serve fresh and hot.

★

NANNIE'S PRUNE CAKE

YIELD: 1 LARGE TUBE CAKE

2 cups unbleached white flour
1 teaspoon cinnamon
1 teaspoon nutmeg
1 teaspoon allspice
1 teaspoon baking soda
1½ cups fructose
1 cup oil
3 eggs
1 teaspoon vanilla extract
1 cup sour milk (see Sour Milk)

1 cup chopped pitted prunes
1 cup pecans

Topping
1 cup raw turbinado sugar
½ cup sour milk
½ teaspoon baking soda
½ teaspoon vanilla extract
½ cup unsalted margarine or butter

1 Preheat oven to 350°.
2 Sift together flour, cinnamon, nut-meg, allspice, baking soda, and fructose. Set aside.
3 In a mixer, cream oil and eggs.
4 Add vanilla extract, then alternate sour milk and sifted dry ingredi-ents, a little at a time, until all of each has been added to the mixture.
5 Stir in chopped pitted prunes and chopped pecans, but do not overmix.
6 Oil and flour tube or fluted tube pan. Pour in batter, tapping bottom

of pan on countertop to settle out bubbles.
7 Bake in preheated 350° oven 55 minutes.
8 While cake is baking, prepare top-ping by combining topping ingre-dients and cooking in a saucepan about 5 minutes over low heat.
9 When cake is done, remove from oven and immediately pour topping over hot cake.
10 Allow cake to cool 20 or 30 min-utes before removing from pan.

★

AUNT ILA'S PUMPKIN CAKE

A simple, old-fashioned family recipe.

YIELD: 1 LARGE TUBE CAKE

1 cup shortening
3 cups fructose
3 large eggs
2 cups fresh pureed or canned pumpkin (1-pound can)
3 cups unbleached white flour
2 teaspoons low-sodium baking powder or 1 teaspoon regular baking powder

1 teaspoon baking soda
1 teaspoon allspice
1 teaspoon cinnamon
1 teaspoon nutmeg
1 teaspoon vanilla extract
1 cup chopped pecans

1 Preheat oven to 350°.
2 Cream shortening, fructose, eggs, and pumpkin in a mixing bowl.
3 In another bowl, sift together flour, baking powder, baking soda, all-spice, cinnamon, and nutmeg.
4 Add sifted ingredients to creamed mixture and mix until blended.

5 Add vanilla extract and chopped pecans.
6 Grease and flour a tube pan and fill with batter. Tap pan on countertop to settle air bubbles.
7 Bake in 350° oven 1½ hours.

★

C O N F E T T I   T O R T E

Sarah Sutton

YIELD: 1 LARGE 4-LAYER TORTE

8 eggs
1½ cups cake flour
¾ cup sugar
¼ cup cold water
1 tablespoon lemon juice
1 teaspoon vanilla extract
1 teaspoon cream of tartar
¼ teaspoon salt

Nougat
2 cups sugar
2 tablespoons lemon juice
¾ cup toasted almonds

Cream
2 cups whipping cream
2 tablespoons sugar
2 teaspoons vanilla extract
¼ cup toasted slivered almonds for trim

1 Preheat oven to 350°.
2 Separate eggs, yolks in one bowl and whites in another.
3 In a large mixing bowl, combine cake flour and sugar. Make an indentation or well in the middle of the mixture.
4 Add egg yolks, cold water, lemon juice, and vanilla extract to the well. Beat until smooth.
5 In a copper bowl or other suitable container, beat egg whites, cream of tartar, salt, and sugar until stiff.
6 Fold egg white mixture into batter. Pour batter into an ungreased tube pan.
7 Bake at 350° for 55 to 60 minutes. Invert pan on rack to cool.
8 When cake is completely cool, re-move from pan, slice into 4 layers, and set aside.
9 To prepare nougat, combine sugar and lemon juice in a heavy skillet. Melt over low heat, stirring occasionally. When the mixture becomes a deep golden color, stir in nuts and pour into a greased pan. Allow to dry, break into pieces, and crush in a food processor.
10 Combine whipping cream, sugar, and vanilla extract in a chilled bowl and whip until firm.
11 Spread whipped cream on sides and top of each layer of cake. Sprinkle nougat between layers and on sides.
12 Trim with toasted slivered almonds and serve.

PIES, TARTS, AND PASTRIES

★

PIE CRUST DOUGH

YIELD: PASTRY FOR
ONE 9-INCH CRUST

2 cups sifted flour
¼ cup unsalted margarine or butter
¼ cup vegetable shortening

4–5 tablespoons ice water
1 egg, beaten

1 Sift and measure flour and combine with margarine or butter in food processor fitted with steel blade.
2 Blend for a short time until mixture looks like cornmeal.
3 Add shortening and blend again until mixture resembles small peas.
4 With the food processor running, add ice water a tablespoonful at a time until the dough forms a ball.
5 Remove dough from food processor bowl and let rest in refrigerator a few minutes.

6 Roll out dough with rolling pin and fit it into pie pan. Brush dough with beaten egg and bake and/or add filling.

Hand Method
Cut butter into tablespoon-size pieces before blending with fork or pastry blender, and blend with fork when adding ice water.

★

MERINGUE FOR PIE

YIELD: MERINGUE FOR
ONE 9- OR 10-INCH PIE

6 egg whites
pinch of salt
pinch of cream of tartar

2 tablespoons fructose or honey
1 teaspoon vanilla extract

1 In a copper bowl or other clean mixing bowl, beat egg whites, salt, and cream of tartar with an electric mixer until the mixture begins to froth.
2 Add fructose or honey and vanilla

extract and continue whipping until meringue forms soft peaks. Do not let peaks become stiff because meringue will be hard to spread on pie.

★

COCONUT CREAM PIE

YIELD: ONE 9- OR 10-INCH PIE

4 egg yolks
½ cup unbleached white flour
¾ cup fructose
3 cups low-fat milk
1 tablespoon cornstarch
2 tablespoons water
3 cups plus 1 tablespoon shredded coconut

1 tablespoon unsalted margarine or butter
2 teaspoons vanilla extract
1 baked pie shell
Meringue for Pie (page 199)

1 Preheat oven to 375°.
2 Separate eggs, reserve whites for meringue, and whip yolks in a small bowl.
3 Blend together cornstarch and water.
4 In a large saucepan blend together flour, fructose, and milk. Simmer over low heat, stirring constantly.
5 Stir cornstarch and water into simmering custard.
6 Bring to a boil, boil 2 minutes, and remove from heat.
7 Dribble a teaspoonful of hot custard into egg yolks and blend thoroughly. Repeat several times.

8 Dribble egg-custard mixture into custard, stir thoroughly, and return to heat.
9 Bring back to a low boil for 1 minute and remove from heat.
10 Stir in 3 cups coconut, margarine or butter, and vanilla extract.
11 Pour into prebaked pie shell and cover with meringue, making sure meringue adheres to edge of crust.
12 Bake at 375° for 12 minutes. Sprinkle top of pie with remaining 1 tablespoon coconut a few minutes before it is done. Pie will slice better if allowed to cool.

★

BUTTERSCOTCH WALNUT CREAM PIE

YIELD: ONE 9-INCH PIE

¾ cup raw turbinado sugar or brown sugar
¼ cup unbleached white flour
¼ teaspoon salt
1¼ cups milk, scalded
3 egg yolks
2 tablespoons unsalted margarine or butter

½ teaspoon vanilla extract
½ cup chopped walnuts
1 baked 9-inch pie shell
Meringue for Pie (page 199) or ½ pint whipping cream, whipped with 2 tablespoons fructose and 1 teaspoon vanilla

1 In the top section of a double boiler, combine sugar, flour, and salt.

2 Scald milk and whisk into sugar and flour mixture. Place top section of double boiler over boiling water and cook 10 minutes, stirring constantly. Remove top section from heat.

3 Separate eggs and reserve whites for meringue or other purposes. Slightly beat yolks and dribble in a small amount of hot butterscotch mixture. When blended, add about half of the hot custard and beat until smooth.

4 Pour egg-custard mixture into remaining hot custard, stir thoroughly, and place over boiling water again. Cook over low heat until mixture thickens (1 to 3 minutes). Do not allow to scorch. Remove from heat.

5 Stir in margarine or butter, vanilla extract, and chopped walnuts.

6 Pour into baked pie shell.

7 Top with meringue and brown, or cool pie and top with whipped cream.

★

BOURBON-LEMON MERINGUE PIE

YIELD: ONE 9-INCH PIE

½ cup fructose
5 tablespoons cornstarch
1½ cups water
3 egg yolks
3 tablespoons unsalted margarine or butter

1 tablespoon finely grated lemon rind
½ cup lemon juice
2 tablespoons bourbon
1 baked 9-inch pie shell
Meringue for Pie (page 199)

1 Preheat oven to 400°.

2 Combine fructose and cornstarch in a 2-quart saucepan.

3 Place saucepan over moderately low heat and gradually stir in water. Heat until mixture thickens and boils. Boil and stir 1 minute, then remove from heat.

4 Beat egg yolks well and dribble in about half of the hot mixture, beating constantly.

5 When egg mixture is smooth, blend it into remaining sauce in pan and stir thoroughly.

6 Return pan to heat, bring to a simmer, and simmer for 1 minute.

7 Remove from heat and stir in margarine or butter, lemon rind, lemon juice, and bourbon. Blend very thoroughly.

8 Pour into baked pie shell and heap with meringue.

9 Bake 10 to 12 minutes. Allow to cool before cutting.

Rum-Lime Meringue Pie
Substitute rum for bourbon, and lime juice and lime peel for lemon.

★

ALL-AMERICAN APPLE PIE

YIELD: ONE 9-INCH PIE

Pie Crust Dough (page 199)
  for 2 crusts
8 apples
¼ cup flour
1 teaspoon cinnamon
juice of 1 lemon
1 cup brown sugar

¼ cup honey
1 tablespoon vanilla extract
1 teaspoon almond extract
1 teaspoon ground cloves
1 egg, beaten
1 tablespoon unsalted margarine or
  butter

1 Preheat oven to 425°.
2 Make pie crust dough for two crusts and line 9-inch pie pan with half of the dough.
3 Slice apples thinly, with or without peeling, into a large bowl.
4 Add all remaining ingredients except margarine or butter and egg.

5 Pour into pie shell and cover with lattice pie crust. Dot with margarine or butter and brush with beaten egg.
6 Bake in preheated 425° oven approximately 1 hour.

★

PEACH COBBLER

The favorite dessert of my childhood, made with my favorite Texas fruit.

YIELD: ONE 13-BY-9-INCH COBBLER

Filling
8 cups peeled, sliced fresh peaches
⅓ cup unbleached white flour
2 tablespoons cornstarch
1 cup fructose
1 tablespoon vanilla extract
1 teaspoon almond extract
juice of ½ lemon
2 teaspoons cinnamon
½ teaspoon ground cloves
½ teaspoon nutmeg

Crust
Pie Crust Dough (page 199)
  for 1 crust
1 tablespoon fructose
1 egg, beaten
2 tablespoons unsalted margarine
  or butter

1 Preheat oven to 400°.
2 Combine all filling ingredients and pour into lightly greased 9-by-13-inch pan.

3 Roll out pie crust dough and cut into strips as shown in figure 15a. Weave strips into a lattice pie crust (figures 15b–15d).

4 Brush crust with beaten egg, sprinkle with fructose, and dot with tiny pieces of margarine or butter.

5 Bake 15 minutes at 400°, then reduce heat to 350° and bake 30 minutes or until crust is golden and filling is baked.

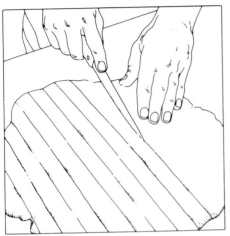

Figure 15a

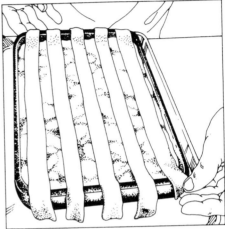

Figure 15b

Figure 15c

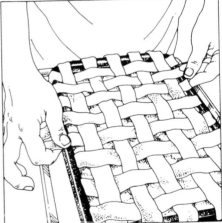

Figure 15d

★

TEXAS HONEY PECAN PIE

YIELD: ONE 9- OR 10-INCH PIE

Pie Crust Dough (page 199)
  for 1 crust
1 cup raw turbinado sugar
2 whole eggs
2 egg whites
1 cup Texas wildflower honey or
  other light, delicate honey
1 tablespoon unsalted margarine or
  butter

¼ cup cream
2 tablespoons Southern Comfort
  liqueur
2 tablespoons unbleached white
  flour
¼ teaspoon nutmeg
¼ teaspoon allspice
¼ teaspoon cinnamon
1¼ cups native Texas pecan halves

1 Preheat oven to 425°.
2 Prepare pie dough. Line pie pan, trim, and flute edge of pastry.
3 Cream together sugar, eggs, and egg whites.
4 Add the following and beat well after each addition: honey, margarine or butter, cream, Southern Comfort liqueur, flour, nutmeg, allspice, and cinnamon.

5 Arrange pecan halves in pastry-lined pie pan.
6 Pour filling gently over pecans.
7 Place pie on middle shelf of preheated oven and cook 15 minutes at 425°. Then reduce heat to 350° and cook 35 to 45 more minutes. Filling should be solidified when cooked.

★

CENTRAL TEXAS PECAN PIE

Zuma Jones

YIELD: ONE 9- OR 10-INCH PIE

3 eggs
1 cup sugar or fructose
1 cup corn syrup

⅛ teaspoon salt
1 cup broken pecan pieces
1 unbaked 9- or 10-inch pie shell

1 Preheat oven to 300°.
2 Slightly beat eggs and stir in all other ingredients.

3 When mixture is blended, pour into unbaked pie shell and bake about 1 hour at 300°.

★

TART PASTRY

YIELD: PASTRY FOR
ONE 10-INCH TART

2 cups sifted flour
3 tablespoons fructose
¼ cup unsalted margarine or butter

¼ cup vegetable shortening
2 eggs
3–4 tablespoons ice water

1 Sift together flour and fructose. Combine with margarine or butter in food processor fitted with steel blade.
2 Blend for a short time until mixture looks like cornmeal.
3 Add vegetable shortening and blend again until mixture resembles small peas.
4 Add 1 beaten egg and blend for 30 seconds.
5 With the food processor running, add ice water a tablespoonful at a time until the dough forms a ball.
6 Remove dough from food processor bowl and let rest in refrigerator a few minutes.

7 Roll out dough with rolling pin and fit into pie pan. Brush dough with remaining beaten egg and bake and/ or add filling.
8 To bake crust before filling, prick bottom of crust with fork (or weight with commercial pie weights or dried beans) and bake at 400° for 15 minutes.

Hand Method

Cut butter into tablespoon-size pieces before blending with fork or pastry blender, and blend with fork when adding ice water.

★

RASPBERRY TART

YIELD: ONE 10-INCH TART

1 baked 10-inch tart pastry shell
2 pints fresh raspberries

½ cup apricot jam
¼ cup black raspberry liqueur

1 Bake tart pastry and cool.
2 Arrange raspberries tightly in a single layer in pastry.
3 In a small saucepan, heat apricot jam, stirring often. Strain jam through a sieve.
4 Mix strained jam with liqueur, and

spoon and brush this glaze across top of raspberries. Work gently so as not to disturb berries.
5 Tart can be served immediately as is or with whipped cream or vanilla ice cream.

★

PEACH TART

YIELD: ONE 10-INCH TART

¾ cup peach preserves
6–8 medium peaches (about 3 cups sliced)

¼ cup fructose
1 baked tart pastry shell

1 Simmer preserves and strain, reserving ½ cup liquid for glazing tart.
2 Slice peaches very thin, combine with fructose, and allow to stand 5 to 10 minutes.

3 Arrange peaches in a circular pattern in tart shell.
4 Brush with warm peach glaze.
5 When ready to serve, garnish with fresh mint leaves and serve with a dollop of yogurt or whipped cream.

★

BAKLAVA

Sarah Sutton

YIELD: 1 LARGE PAN

1 pound phillo dough leaves (available at specialty stores)
1 cup unsalted margarine or butter, melted
2 cups chopped walnuts
½ cup sugar
1 tablespoon rose water

Syrup
2 cups sugar
1 cup water
2–3 drops lemon juice
1 teaspoon rose water

1 Preheat oven to 350°.
2 Using a soft pastry brush, brush the bottom and sides of a large, deep baking pan (about 12 by 17 inches) with melted margarine or butter.
3 Layer the phillo leaves, 2 at a time, brushing every second leaf with melted margarine or butter. Use half the leaves (about 12) in this manner.
4 Mix together chopped walnuts, ½ cup sugar, and 1 tablespoon rose water. Spread this mixture over layered dough.

5 Layer remaining phillo leaves as in step 3.
6 Cut baklava diagonally to form diamonds before baking.
7 Bake 30 to 45 minutes at 350° until golden.
8 To make syrup, combine sugar, water, and lemon juice in a medium-sized saucepan. Boil 15 minutes over medium heat.
9 Remove syrup from heat and add rose water. Pour syrup over warm baklava.

FRUIT AND SPECIALTY DESSERTS

★

BAKED APPLES WITH CURRANTS

YIELD: 6 SERVINGS

6 firm cooking apples
juice of 1 lemon
4 tablespoons unsalted margarine
  or butter

6 tablespoons currants
6 tablespoons raw turbinado sugar
2 tablespoons brandy
2 tablespoons cinnamon

1 Preheat oven to 350°.
2 Wash and core apples and remove peel from top third of each. Sprinkle with lemon juice to prevent discoloration.
3 Grease a baking dish with 2 tablespoons margarine or butter and place apples in dish.
4 Combine currants, sugar, brandy, cinnamon, and 1 tablespoon softened margarine or butter.
5 Stuff apples with currant and sugar mixture and dot top of fruit with bits of remaining tablespoon of margarine or butter.
6 Bake 30 minutes in 350° oven. Increase heat to 400° and bake 5 more minutes.

★

PEARS BAKED IN PASTRY

YIELD: 4 SERVINGS

4 medium-ripe pears (Anjou,
  Bartlett, or Bosc)
4 tablespoons fructose

4 teaspoons cinnamon
1 recipe Tart Pastry (page 205)
¹⁄₃ cup cream

1 Preheat oven to 400°.
2 Select pears that have long stems still intact. Carefully peel and remove about half of core by scraping out from bottom of fruit.
3 Combine fructose and cinnamon and roll peeled pears in mixture until well coated.
4 Roll out pastry on floured surface and cut into four 5-inch squares.
Cut a small hole in the middle of each square. Carefully place squares of pastry over pears, folding and smoothing pastry and tucking excess into cavity of pear.
5 Brush lightly with cream and decorate with leaves cut from pastry scraps if desired.
6 Bake on buttered cookie sheet at 400° for 10 minutes, then reduce

heat to 375° and cook 30 minutes longer. If top of pastry begins to scorch before lower half is done, lay a piece of aluminum foil over

pears for remainder of cooking time.

7 Serve warm or at room temperature.

★

FRESH FRUIT AND TOFU PUREE

Quick, low-calorie, and surprisingly satisfying.

YIELD: 6 SERVINGS

2½ *cups strawberries, pineapple, or other fresh fruit*
12 ounces tofu
¼ *cup honey*

½ *teaspoon vanilla extract*
1 tablespoon orange liqueur
freshly grated nutmeg
mint for garnish

1 Prepare fresh fruit and puree in a blender or food processor.
2 Add tofu, honey, vanilla extract, and orange liqueur and puree until well blended.

3 Spoon into individual serving dishes and chill 1 hour.
4 Garnish with nutmeg and mint.

★

CHOCOLATE MOUSSE

Carl Manz

YIELD: 8 SERVINGS

12 ounces semisweet chocolate
7 eggs
1 orange

1 teaspoon vanilla extract
1 pint whipping cream
4 tablespoons sugar

1 Place water in the bottom of a double boiler; in the top part, place the chocolate. Place double boiler over low heat and stir occasionally until chocolate is completely melted.
2 While chocolate is melting, separate eggs and grate and juice orange. Mix grated orange peel and juice into egg yolks and set aside.
3 Whip cream with vanilla extract and 2 tablespoons sugar until it forms stiff peaks. Set aside.

4 Whip egg whites, slowly adding remaining 2 tablespoons sugar, until they stand in stiff peaks.
5 Stir chocolate together with egg yolks.
6 Fold in half of the whipped cream and a quarter of the egg whites.
7 Gently fold in remaining egg whites.
8 Ladle mousse mixture into serving cups and refrigerate at least 1 hour. At serving time, top each with a dab of remaining whipped cream.

★

HONEY CUSTARD

Betty Wertz

YIELD: 4 SERVINGS

¼ *teaspoon salt (optional)*
3 eggs
¼ *cup honey*

2 cups scalded milk
nutmeg

1 Preheat oven to 325°.
2 Add salt to eggs and beat just enough to combine whites and yolks.
3 Add honey to scalded milk and pour slowly into egg mixture while stirring.
4 Pour into 1-quart baking dish; sprinkle with nutmeg.

5 Place baking dish in a larger pan containing enough hot water to rise an inch or so up the sides of the dish. Place both pans in oven and bake at 325° about 40 minutes or until firm.

★

STRAWBERRY FLUFF SORBET

YIELD: 6 – 8 SERVINGS

3 pints fresh strawberries
5 egg whites
pinch of cream of tartar
¾ *cup fructose or 9 packages Equal*

3 tablespoons orange liqueur
1 teaspoon vanilla extract
candied rose petals for garnish
fresh mint leaves for garnish

1 Wash strawberries and remove stems. Puree in a blender 2 cups at a time. Place into a large bowl and set in refrigerator to chill.
2 In a copper bowl or a clean mixing bowl, whip egg whites with cream of tartar until soft peaks begin to form. Sprinkle in fructose, several tablespoons at a time, until meringue forms stiff peaks. Set aside.
3 Remove strawberries from refriger-

ator and stir in orange liqueur and vanilla extract.
4 Stir in a quarter of the egg whites to lighten the mixture, and then fold in the remainder.
5 Freeze mixture in a 6-quart ice cream freezer. (See *Frozen Desserts* if ice cream freezer is not available.) Serve in chilled bowls, garnished with candied rose petals and mint leaves.

★

FRESH RASPBERRY SORBET

YIELD: 6–8 SERVINGS

3 pints fresh raspberries
1 cup fructose or 12 packages Equal
1 teaspoon vanilla extract

juice of 1 lemon
½ bottle cold champagne

1 Rinse, puree, and sieve raspberries.
2 Mix with fructose, vanilla extract, and lemon juice. Chill in refrigerator 30 minutes.
3 Remove from refrigerator and add champagne.
4 Freeze in sorbet machine or ice cream freezer according to machine instructions. (See *Frozen Desserts* if ice cream freezer or sorbet machine is not available.)
5 Allow to thaw slightly before serving.

★

FROZEN PEACH KEFIR

YIELD: 6–8 SERVINGS

1 quart peach kefir
2 cups fresh or frozen peaches
1 tablespoon fructose

2 teaspoons Amaretto liqueur
fresh mint leaves for garnish

1 Chop peaches coarsely and combine with all other ingredients.
2 Freeze in sorbet machine or ice cream freezer according to machine instructions. (See *Frozen Desserts* if ice cream freezer or sorbet machine is not available.)
3 Serve in chilled dishes and garnish with fresh mint.

★

BANANA-STRAWBERRY SORBET

YIELD: 8–10 SERVINGS

6 ripe bananas
2 pints ripe strawberries
1 tablespoon raspberry liqueur

juice of ½ lime
1 teaspoon fructose

1 Puree all ingredients together in a blender or food processor.
2 Chill 1 hour in refrigerator.
3 Freeze 25 minutes in a sorbet machine or ice cream freezer. (See *Frozen Desserts* if sorbet machine or ice cream freezer is not available.)

11

BEVERAGES

NONALCOHOLIC BEVERAGES

★

GRAPEFRUIT JUICE SPRITZER

Refreshing, nonalcoholic, and low-calorie.

cold fresh-squeezed grapefruit juice
chilled sparkling water such as Ramlösa, Perrier, or Artesia
slices of fresh lime for garnish

1 Mix equal parts of grapefruit juice and sparkling water.

2 Serve garnished with lime slices, either on the rocks or straight up.

★

HOT SPICED CHERRY CIDER

YIELD: 4 SERVINGS

1 quart cherry cider
6 cinnamon sticks
6 whole allspice berries

10 whole cloves
juice of ½ lemon
slices of lemon for garnish

1 Place all ingredients except lemon slices in a large pan. Bring to a simmer over medium heat.
2 Remove from heat and allow to sit covered for 30 minutes.

3 Strain out spices.
4 When ready to serve, reheat and serve hot with a slice of lemon in each mug.

★

QUICK WATERMELON JUICE

Pamela Navarez

YIELD: 2 SERVINGS

enough cold watermelon, rind removed, to fill a 1-quart blender jar
wedges of watermelon for garnish

1 Fill blender jar with cold melon, seeds and all.
2 Thoroughly blend 2 to 3 minutes.

3 Strain into serving glasses and garnish with a small wedge of watermelon.

★

EL PASO HORCHATA

Pamela Navarez

This unusual seed milk recipe was adapted by Pamela Navarez from that of her abuelita *(little grandmother).*

YIELD: ABOUT 1 QUART

dried seeds from 3 cantaloupes
1 tablespoon fructose
½ teaspoon cinnamon

½ teaspoon vanilla extract
1 quart cold water

1 Scrape out seeds from fresh melons, including as little pulp as possible. The pulp tends to sour during the drying process.
2 Place fresh seeds into a strainer or colander and rinse thoroughly under cold running water.
3 Spread rinsed seeds evenly around the sides of the colander or strainer, and allow to dry for 24 hours.
4 Pick through and collect dried seeds, avoiding bits of pulp. If desired, seeds can be stored in a sealed container in the refrigerator for future use.
5 Place dried cantaloupe seeds, fructose, cinnamon, vanilla extract, and cold water in a blender.
6 Blend 3 minutes until very smooth and strain into a jar or pitcher. Serve cold.

★

BURNT ALMOND COFFEE

A coffee grinder is required for this recipe.

YIELD: 1 QUART

¼ cup whole almonds
¼ cup good-quality coffee beans

1 Preheat oven to 400°.
2 Toast almonds on a baking sheet until they are a deep rich brown. Remove from oven and cool.
3 Combine almonds and coffee beans and grind together.
4 Prepare ground mixture with 1 quart of water as you would any other coffee.

★

MINT LEAF TEA

Herbal teas both hot and cold are even better if the herbs are fresh from one's own garden. Root and bark teas are usually simmered to bring out their potency, while leaf and flower herbs are most often simply steeped in a teapot, as with any fine tea. This mint tea recipe provides a good basic outline to follow with other herbs, dried and fresh.

YIELD: 1 SERVING PER CUP OF WATER

1 Heat to boiling enough water and then some.
2 Put a cup or more of water in a nice teapot to warm it. Allow to sit a couple of minutes.
3 Pour out water and put in 1 tablespoon dried mint per serving plus 1 "for the pot." With fresh mint, simply fill teapot with a handful of washed green mint.

4 Bring water in kettle back to boiling and pour into teapot with herbs. Cover and steep 7 to 10 minutes.
5 Strain and enjoy hot or chilled. Herbal teas can, of course, be garnished with lemons, limes, oranges, or sprigs of herb. Sweeteners should be used very sparingly, if at all, so as not to obscure the distinctive herbal flavors.

★

SASSAFRAS ROOT TEA

A widely known spring tonic. The sassafras plant also provides the dried and powdered leaves that are the legendary filé for gumbo, a seasoning first introduced to the Louisiana settlers by the Choctaw Indians.

YIELD: 4 SERVINGS

3–4 small sections of sassafras root (each about the size of a finger)
8 cups water

1 Add sassafras root sections to cold water, bring to a simmer, and simmer for 30 minutes.

2 Strain and serve, or chill for iced tea.

ALCOHOLIC BEVERAGES

★

SUMMER PUNCH
YIELD: 8 SERVINGS

1 fifth good extra dry champagne
2 pints fresh or frozen raspberries

1 quart fresh grapefruit juice
fresh mint for garnish

1 Chill champagne for 24 hours.
2 Puree raspberries with grapefruit juice and strain. Place juice in a covered container and chill at least 2 hours.
3 Chill punch bowl or whatever container you wish to use. Chill champagne glasses.

4 Wash and prepare fresh sprigs of mint.
5 When ready to serve punch, blend together champagne and juice in chilled punch bowl.
6 Pour into chilled champagne glasses and garnish with sprigs of fresh mint.

★

KIR ROYALE PUNCH
YIELD: 8 SERVINGS

2 fifths good extra dry champagne
2 pints fresh or frozen blackberries
¼ cup crème de cassis or Chambord liqueur

lemon zest for garnish

1 Chill champagne for 24 hours.
2 Puree blackberries with liqueur and strain. Place liquid in a covered container and chill at least 2 hours.
3 Chill punch bowl or whatever container you wish to use. Chill champagne glasses.
4 Cut lemon zest (small, thin strips of lemon peel).

5 When ready to serve punch, blend together champagne and berry-liqueur mixture in chilled punch bowl.
6 Pour into chilled champagne glasses and garnish with lemon zest.

★

BRANDY FREEZE
YIELD: 6 SERVINGS

1 pint fine coffee ice cream
½ cup half-and-half
½ cup coffee liqueur

½ cup brandy
½ cup crushed ice
grated nutmeg

1 Combine all ingredients except nutmeg in blender and blend thoroughly.

2 Pour into chilled glasses and top with freshly grated nutmeg.

★

TEXAS LIQUID GOLD MARGARITA
YIELD: 1 SERVING

1½ ounces Cuervo Gold tequila
1½ ounces Grand Marnier liqueur
1½ ounces freshly squeezed lime juice

¼ cup crushed ice
saucer of coarse salt (optional)
slice of lime for garnish

1 Combine tequila, liqueur, and lime juice with ice in blender jar. Blend at high speed 1 minute.
2 Rub rim of glass with lime peel and dip into a saucer of salt. (This step may be omitted.)
3 Pour margarita into glass, garnish with lime slice, and serve.